HARVEY FIERSTEIN *AND* SUSAN EDWARDS

Photo Credits: © *Gerry Goodstein*

TORCH SONG TRILOGY

three plays by

HARVEY FIERSTEIN

*with a note from
the Author*

VILLARD BOOKS   **NEW YORK**

For Paul Reese

. . . and with loving memories of Kenn Hill,
Charles Embry, Bud Sherman,
J. Galen McKinley and my Father

The author wishes to thank the following people for their help and inspiration: Ray Benkoczy, Helen Hanft, Paul Falzone, Mitchell Maxwell, Helen Merrill, Harvey Tavel, Ronald Tavel, Dorothea Regal, Norman Glick, George Whitmore, Don Shewey, Richard Hale, and a very special thank you to the two people most responsible for bringing this Trilogy to life: Eric Concklin and my "Mama" Ellen Stewart.

TORCH SONG TRILOGY *was presented on Broadway at the Little Theatre on June 10, 1982 by Kenneth Waissman, Martin Markinson, John Glines, Lawrence Lane, BetMar and Donald Tick with the following cast:*

ARNOLD	Harvey Fierstein
ED	Court Miller
LADY BLUES	Susan Edwards
LAUREL	Diane Tarleton
ALAN	Paul Joynt
DAVID	Fisher Stevens
MRS. BECKOFF	Estelle Getty

Directed by Peter Pope
Original Score by Ada Janik
Stage Design by Bill Stabile
Musical Direction by Ned Levy
Costumes by Mardi Philips
Lighting by Scott Pinkney
Production Stage Manager: Herb Vogler

Author's Note

I have been blessed with seven honest, earnest, free-tongued characters who, within these pages, willingly impart more of themselves to you than the closest friends would ever dare. I will therefore leave them to their storytelling with the briefest of Parental Guidance.

Like a gaudy East Indian purse; outrageous in color, embroidered in cliche design, the worth of these plays lies ultimately in the tiny mirrors woven into the fabric wherein we catch our reflections. Perhaps you'll see a little of yourself on the phone with Arnold's "Why don't you love me anymore?" call. Or maybe find yourself in Laurel's "Just because I said that's what I want doesn't mean that I'm ready for it" logic. Or it might be while reading Mrs. Beckoff you'll stop and smile, "That's *my* Mother." Any little thng that makes you feel less alone is what and why these plays are.

Not one of the characters you'll meet is "right." There are no answers forthcoming. But like an old familiar half heard song playing on a jukebox you might just catch a line that reaches out and touches something going on inside of you. And for that instant you are relieved of the isolation. That is the worth of a Torch Song. That is the goal of these plays.

The International Stud

INTERNATIONAL STUD was first presented by La Mama E.T.C. on
February 2, 1978 with the following cast:

LADY BLUES	*Diane Tarleton*
ARNOLD	*Harvey Fierstein*
ED	*Steve Spiegel*

Directed by Eric Concklin
Musical Direction by Ned Levy
Costumes by Mardi Philips
Lighting by Joanna Schielke
Production Stage Manager: B.J. Allen
The production subsequently played at The Player's Theatre with Richard
Dow as ED and Lee Evans as Stage Manager.

There is a gay bar in New York City called "The International Stud." It
boasts a pool table, pinball machine and the jumpingest backroom in town.
I dearly dedicate these plays to all who made it their home.

I wish for each of them the courage to leave it when they can, and the
good sense to come back when they must.

CHARACTERS
Ed Reiss: Thirty-four, very handsome; masculine with a boyish charm.
Arnold: Twenty-four (going on forty). A Kvetch of great wit and want.
Lady Blues

SYNOPSIS OF SCENES
1) January. Arnold, backstage of a nightclub.
2) February. Ed in "The International Stud" bar.
3) June. Ed and Arnold in their respective apartments.
4) September. Arnold in "The International Stud" bar.
5) November. Ed and Arnold backstage.

LADY BLUES

Before scene 1 and between each of the following scenes, Lady Blues appears on a separate set, atop a grand piano, dressed in period, and sings a 1920s or 30s torch song in the manner of Helen Morgan or Ruth Etting. The choice of songs I leave to the director, as they should highlight the values of each particular production. They should not comment on the action as much as conjure it . . .

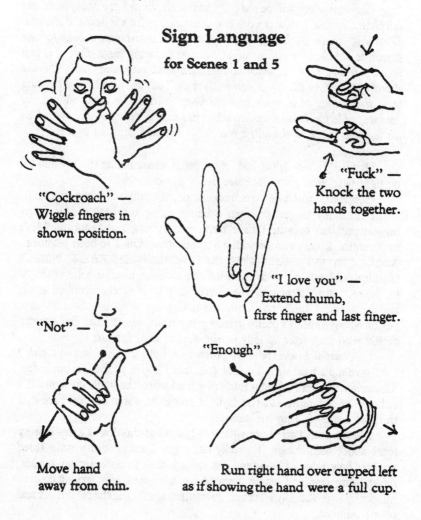

Sign Language

for Scenes 1 and 5

"Cockroach" — Wiggle fingers in shown position.

"Fuck" — Knock the two hands together.

"I love you" — Extend thumb, first finger and last finger.

"Not" — Move hand away from chin.

"Enough" — Run right hand over cupped left as if showing the hand were a full cup.

Scene 1: Arnold

The play is performed against a black cyclorama with as little actual scenery as possible. Upstage center the grand piano sits on its platform raising the singer high above the action. Downstage of her, on either side, are three-foot high platforms which will be the two apartments. Each has a chair, table and telephone. Arnold's chair is worn and comfortable, Ed's is new and straight. Downstage center stands the "Stud" platform. It is just large enough for one person to stand comfortably, raised two feet from the stage. Left of it is a larger platform, 6' × 8', which holds an arm chair and vanity table. It is the dressing room. As the lights come down on Lady Blues after her opening song the sounds of a music box are heard softly. The lights rise on the backstage platform revealing Arnold in full drag applying a false eyelash to his face. He turns off the music box . . . The lash slips out of place . . .

Damned Elmer's glue! Just let me finish emasculating this eye and I'll be right with you. [*Fixes it. Poses in the mirror.*]

Gorgeous, huh? Use your imagination, it's still under construction.

I think my biggest problem is being young and beautiful. It is my biggest problem because I have never been young and beautiful. More importantly, I will never be young and beautiful. Oh, I've been beautiful. And God knows I've been young. But never the twain have met. Not so's anyone would notice anyway. A shrink acquaintance of mine believes this to be the root of my attraction to a class of men most subtly described as old and ugly. But I think he's underestimating my wheedles. See, an ugly person who goes after a pretty person gets nothing but trouble. But a pretty person who goes after an ugly person gets at least cab-fare.

I ain't sayin' I never fell for a pretty face, but when *"les jeux sont faits"* . . . give me a toad with a pot of gold and I'll give ya three meals a day. 'Cause honeys, ain't no such thing as a toad when the lights go down. It's either feast or famine. It's the daylight you gotta watch out for. Face it, a thing of beauty is a joy 'till sunrise.

I never push Lady Luck myself. I got, what'choo call a extra-sensory sense about such things. If I really like a guy I automatically wake three minutes before him. Giving me just enough time to unsucker my pucker, reinstate my coif, and repose my repose so's his eyes upon waking conjure images by Jove and Lana Turner; guaranteeing my breakfast if not his real phone number.

Here's another hint to all present presently unattached. You can cross any man off your dance card who A: Discusses his wonderful relationship with his mother. B: Discusses his wonderful relationship with his shrinker. Or C: Refuses to discuss his wonderful relationship with his mother or shrinker. See, a guy who's got that kind of confidante is in what I call a "state of confession." And experience has sorely taught me, you can never be more to a man in such a state than subject matter for their conversations . . .

Not that I got anything against analysis, I don't. I think it's a great way to keep from boring your friends. But what's good for the bored just ain't so for the bed, if you get my drift. See, when there's trouble in Paradise you got two possible M.O.'s. Pull back or push in. But pull back when he's got a professional shoulder to lean on and the entire effect of losing you is shot. Try pushing and you've bought yourself two for one. Push hard enough, and you'll find yourself visiting him Sundays at the "Happy Home For The Bewildered."

Now, I ain't sayin' you should only date sane men (I don't want to kill off all the fish in the polluted sea), but at least find one who's willing to fight on his own. Give me a man with both fists clenched tight . . . and I'll give you a smile from here to next Thursday.

And there's another group you've gotta watch your food stamps around . . . "The Hopeless." They break down into three major categories: Married, "Just in for the Weekend," and terminally ill. Those affairs are the worst. You go into them with your eyes open, knowing all the limitations and accepting them maturely . . . then wham bam! . . . you're writing letters to Dear Abby and burning black candles at midnight and you ask yourself, "What happened?" I'll tell you what happened. You got just what you wanted! The person who thinks they's mature enough to handle an affair that's hopeless from the beginning is the very same person who keeps the publishers of Gothic Romances up to their tragic endings in mink; not to mention the reissuers of those twenties torch ditties . . . Music to be miserable by.

So, what's left? I don't know. But there are some. I found one once. His name was Charley. He was tall, handsome, rich, deaf. Everything you could want in an affair and more. The deafness was the more. He never screamed at me, all his friends were nice and quiet, I could play music as loud as I liked without ever disturbing his reading, and best of all I could snore. I even learned me some of that sign language. Wait, I still remember some. Like this here, [*He demonstrates*] it means cockroach. And this one [*Demonstrates*] means fuck. Here's my favorite. [*Demonstrates*] It means "I love you." And I did. But . . . [*Signing and speaking together*] not enough. I guess I bought them Gothic publishers a few minks of my own.

[*Back to his dressing*] For those of yis what ain't yet guessed I am an entertainer (or what's left of one), I go by the name Virginia Hamm. Ain't that a kick in the rubber parts? You should hear some of my former handles; Kitty Litter, Lorretta Dung, Bertha Venation . . . and I'm plenty tough too. I can afford to be; behind a phony name, face and figure. But that's alright.

See, I'm among the last of a dying breed. Once the E.R.A. and gay civil rights bills have been passed, me and mine will find ourselves swept under the carpets like the blacks done to Amos, Andy and Aunt Jemima. But that's alright too. With a voice and face like this I got nothing to worry about, I can always drive a cab. And that, chillun', is called power. Be it gay, black or flowered it always comes down to the survival of the majority.

Shit, I'd better get a move on it! [*He takes a roll of toilet paper and unwinds two huge wads.*] Would y'all mind turning your backs? . . . Well, could you at least close your eyes?

[*He places the paper in his bra with his back to the audience, turns proudly with his chest held high, catches the unevenness of the sizes in the mirror and adjusts them.*]

There are easier things in this life than being a drag queen. But, I ain't got no choice. Try as I may, I just can't walk in flats. [*Putting on his hat and shoes*]

You know what I really want? I want the International Stud. No, not the bar. The man. A stud. A guy who knows what he wants and ain't a'scared to go out and get it. A guy who satisfies his every need, and don't mind if you get what you want in the bargain. Matter of fact, he aims to please. He'd be happy to be whatever you wanted him to be, 'cause you're happy bein' what he wants you to be. The more you put in, the more you get back. An honest man. The International Stud. One size fits all. But I wouldn't want no guy that wanted me like this here. No, I'd need him for the rest of the time. For the other part of me. The part that's not so well protected. Oh, there's plenty that want me like this. And I take their admiration gratefully. But, at a distance. I guess a drag queen's like bein' a oil painting! You gotta stand back from it to get the full effect.

[*Standing*] Well, I think we're in business! My, how time flies when you's doin' all the talking. [*Tucking in the chair*] Who knows, maybe my Right Man is out there tonight, right? Y'all take care now, hear? [*He makes the "I love you" sign, turns to go, stops and comes back.*] Ya' know . . . In my life I have slept with more men than are named and/or numbered in the Bible (Old and New Testaments put together). But in all those beds not once has someone said, "Arnold, I love you . . ." that I could believe. So, I ask myself, "Do you really care?" And the only honest answer I can give myself is, "Yes, I care." I care be . . . [*Catches himself*] I care a great deal. But not enough.

 [*He smiles knowingly as the lights black out on him and up on the singer.*]

Scene 2: Ed

As Lady Blues finishes her song, the sounds of a bar are heard faintly and the lights reveal Ed standing on the Stud platform, his back to the audience. He is tall, lean and very handsome. Although he is in his thirties his greatest charm is his boyishness.

[*Suddenly stepping back onto someone's foot*] Oh, excuse me. I'm sorry. I was just trying to duck that pool cue. Gets pretty crowded in here on a Saturday. Your foot O.K.? Good.

[*He turns away, but then can't help sneaking a look at the stranger. He smiles and turns away embarrassed, then turns to him again.*] No permanent damage, I hope. To your foot I mean . . . Good.

[*He turns away again, but still tries to sneak a look behind him. He gathers his courage and confronts the stranger with huge smile.*] Look, the name's Ed Reiss. My friends call me Ed. [*No response*] I'm Saggitarius. . . . What's so funny? . . . Oh, well, some people like to know that stuff. I don't believe in any of it myself, but I have done some reading about it. See, I like to know what's expected of me. [*He stares with a huge grin.*] You have a beautiful smile. . . . No, really, you do. Can I get you another beer?

Alright, One Lite coming up. [*To bartender*] Can I have a Lite please?

No, not a match. I meant a Lite beer. [*To stranger*] Am I speaking English? I feel like I'm a Martian or something. I think it's that smile of yours. Say, what's your name?

Arnold? Your friends call you Arnie or Arn?

Arnold. Well, nice to meet you Arnold. [*Handing money to the bartender*] Here you go. [*Beer to Arnold*] And here you go.

Are you Italian?

Spanish?

Jewish!? I never would have guessed it. Not with those dark romantic eyes. I don't remember ever seeing you here before. I don't get in that often myself. I teach over in Brooklyn and so have to be up and out pretty early, so if I'm feeling horny this is where I come. I can be in and out of the backroom and home in bed within an hour.

No. I'm off tomorrow. That's why I'm out here instead of back there. You really do have beautiful eyes. Are you wearing make-up?

I didn't think so. So, . . . uh . . . how's the backroom? Crowded, I'll bet.

Never?

No, it's just that you don't expect to meet someone in a backroom bar who's never been in the backroom. Are you here with a friend?

Is he your lover?

So, you're unattached. How lucky for me. Where you from?

Sure, I know where that is. Live alone?

Well, look, I have a car . . . I'd ask you back to my place but I have this straight roommate. He's got a hangup about gays. It's really his place. I only sublet from him.

Oh, well, I date women too. So . . . Anyway, I really live upstate. I've got a farm up about an hour from Montreal. That's my real home. I spend the weekends there during the school year and then all of my summer vacation. I own half of Walton Mountain.

No, that's really what it's called. Most of the land is trees, but there's a piece of flat farming land with an old barn and I work a half acre of that. I grow all my own vegetables. I've even got a small vineyard. The mountains have some great white water for canoeing, and in the winter . . . it's a skier's dream. You ski?

Would you like to learn?

Alright, it's a deal. You'll love the house, it's really great. One of those old Victorian farm houses with lots of ginger-bread and Franklin stoves. My father and I are restoring it.

Well, my parents winter in Florida but come north to stay with me in the warmer months. Hey, what'd'ya' say we continue this conversation in the car?

Great. By the way, what do you do?

No, I meant for a living.

Can you really make a living doing that?

I do believe you're the first one I've met . . . personally. Ready? [*Putting on his coat*] The car's just across the street. Anyone ever tell you you have a very sexy voice? You really do. Is it natural or do you have a cold? [*Gesturing*] After you.

[*He turns as the lights go out on the platform and come up on the singer.*]

Radio Show Between

The following conversation should be tape recorded and played during Lady Blues' third song. She should listen to it as if it were part of the musical break. It is underscored by the piano.

ED   [*Excited*] Oh, wow. Your place is really great.

ARNOLD   I'm glad you like it.

ED   No, it's really fabulous. But, would you mind putting on a light?

ARNOLD   There's not much to see.

ED   There's you.

ARNOLD   [*Embarrassed giggle, sound of light switch*] Better?

ED   Better . . . and better. You're shaking.

ARNOLD   Nervous, I guess.

ED   Me too.

ARNOLD   Really?

ED   Really.

ARNOLD   I'm glad you asked me home.

ED   Me too.

ARNOLD   Ed?

ED   Yeah?

ARNOLD   I feel . . . I don't know . . . kind'a scared.

ED   Better?

ARNOLD   Better . . . and better.

          [*They both laugh intimately as Lady Blues continues her song.*]

Scene 3

The lights come up on Arnold in his apartment. He sits on the floor in shorts and a sweat-shirt with a paperback stuck in his mouth. It is The I Ching. *He is throwing coins and marking the hexagram nervously. Reading . . .*

ARNOLD   "Having completed the hexagram, compare it to the chart on page 228." [*He flips to the chart and compares his scratchings to it.*] Here it is. Number thirty-eight. [*He searches excitedly for the right page. He finds it.*] Here we go. "Hexagram Thirty-eight. Koo-eee-iiiii. The Estranged."

          [*He is struck by its meaning, and hides the book under the chair. He lights a cigarette while staring at the phone. He climbs into the chair, grabs the phone into his lap and dials.*] Hello, Murray? Call me back.

          [*He slams down the receiver and freezes, his hand perched over the phone ready to lift it as soon as it rings. It does not. Slowly his face begins to crack with worry. Still the phone does not ring. He is practically in frozen hysteria when suddenly it does ring.*]

ARNOLD   [*Grabbing it angrily*] God dammit, Murray, what took you so long? . . . The shower could have waited Murray. . . . The shampoo in the shower could have waited, Murray. . . . The man with the shampoo in the shower could have waited, Murray. Anyway, I can't talk now. I gotta keep the line free. [*Starting to hang up*] What? . . . I just wanted to make sure the phone was working. . . . Ed. Alright? I'm expecting a call from Ed. . . . When? Well, it is now Tuesday, eight P.M. Well, Ed's gonna call sometime after Tuesday eight P.M. . . . Of course he's gonna call, Murray. You think I'd sit by the phone for six days if he wasn't gonna call? . . . You are getting on my nerves, Murray. Look he is a very busy man. With a great many responsibilities. He will call me when he is able. And I will understand. Got it! When you have been seeing someone for four months, Murray, you build a relationship based on trust and mutual respect. Something you and your Magic fingers shower massage would not understand. He will call, Murray. He knows when he's got a good thing going. He knows I ain't like those other cheap tricks he sees. He knows I got something that puts me above those runned up the mill, always on Sunday, anyplace I hang my crotch is home variety of homosexual commonly cruised in these here parts. I am important, Murray. I am impressive, Murray. But most of all, Murray, I am mysterious. Which is a quality you don't find on every bar stool. [*Getting slow and sexy*] Oh, no, Murray, he will call. And when he does. . . . And when he does . . . And when he does. . . . [*Jumping suddenly*] The phone's gonna be free! [*Slams down the phone*] [*Pouting*] Oh ye of little faith!

[*Arnold gets an idea. He puts out his cigarette, takes the phone in hand, takes two real deep breaths and holds them and dials. The phone in Ed's apartment rings as the lights come up revealing Ed dressed neatly for a date just about to open a bottle of red wine. There are two glasses on the table by the phone.*]

ED   [*Lifting the receiver*] Hello?

ARNOLD   [*Letting out his breath in pants*] Hi. Was that you?

ED   [*Recognizing the voice. Slightly uneasy.*] Oh, hi. Was what me?

ARNOLD   Just now on the phone. Was that you trying to get me?

ED   No.

ARNOLD   Oh. Then I wonder who it was? See, I just walked in this second. [*Non-stop*] You know, I've been out of town all week. And I was fumbling at the door with my luggage and the keys when I heard the phone ringing, so of course I dropped the keys, and when I bent over to pick up the keys I dropped the luggage, so of course since I was nervous and the phone was ringing one of the cases uncaught and opened up and everything fell out all over the place. So, finally I got the door open and kicked everything inside, dove at the phone and picked it up just in time to hear whoever it was calling hang up. [*Slight nervous laugh, then quietly, almost sadly*] So, how are you?

ED   [*Gently*] I was going to call you real soon. I've just been really
            busy.

ARNOLD   What's the difference, we're talking now. By the way, you
            remember that Helen Morgan record I played last time you
            were here? Well, I was able to find another copy in a little
            secondhand shop uptown. It's almost like new. So I picked it
            up for you.

ED   [*Embarrassed*] Thanks.

ARNOLD   You're welcome.

ED   Look, Arnold, I can't talk right now. I've got a friend coming
            over for dinner and uh . . .

ARNOLD   That's O.K. I just called 'cause I thought it was you calling.
            So, give me a call when you're not so busy.

ED   [*Guilty*] I'm sorry. I'll call you tomorrow.

ARNOLD   [*Hurting*] Hey, no problem. I understand.

ED   [*Annoyed suddenly*] What do you understand? You never
            give me a chance to call you. Every time I'm just about to
            there you are calling me.

ARNOLD   [*Frightened*] E.S.P. maybe? [*No response*] Well, just think of
            all the money I save you on phone calls.

ED   [*Gently amused*] You're impossible. You know that?

ARNOLD   [*Relaxing a bit*] Yeah. It's a wonder you put up with me.

ED   [*Checks his watch*] So, how was your trip?

ARNOLD   My trip? Oh, my trip. O.K. Who's coming over for dinner?

ED   A friend. You don't know him.

ARNOLD   How do you know? I know lots of hymns: "Battle Hymn of
            the Republic," "Rock of Ages," "Oh Come Emman-
            uel". . . .

ED   You are impossible.

ARNOLD   So, is it an old him or a new him?

ED   [*Tightening*] Why do you do this to yourself?

ARNOLD   I'm just asking. Can't a person show a little interest in an-
           other person's life?[*Pause*] So?

ED   A new one.

ARNOLD   [*Definitely wounded but smiling through*] Aha. Where'd you
           meet him? The Stud?

ED   I've really got to go now, Arnold. I'll call you soon, alright?

ARNOLD   That's what you said last week.

ED   Well maybe if you waited and gave me a chance to call . . .

ARNOLD   [*Letting go*] That's all I'm asking *you* for; a chance. Why're
           you treating me like some trick you picked up last night?

ED   [*Angry*] Arnold, I don't want a scene on the phone. I'll call
           you tomorrow and we'll get together and talk.

ARNOLD   [*Real soft*] What's wrong? Until last week, I could've sworn
           things were going great for both of us. What's happening?

ED   Not now, Arnold.

ARNOLD   Yes. Now.

ED   Arnold, I'm just going to get angry.

ARNOLD   So get angry! Just talk to me! [*Silence*] Hello? Are you there?

ED   [*Pause. Quietly.*] I'm here.

ARNOLD   [*Soft*] I miss you. [*Pause*] I think about you all the time.
           [*Pause*] I'm so damned horny.

ED   [*Slight laugh*] You need a job.

ARNOLD   I've got a job. I need a lover.

ED   [*Hard*] Well, I don't. There. Is that what you wanted to hear?

ARNOLD   No. But it's a beginning. What *do* you need?

ED   A friend. I've said that all along. If you'd listen sometimes
           instead of . . .

ARNOLD   You've got a friend. And a lover too. All in one neat package.
           That's modern efficiency at work.

ED   It is not what I need.

ARNOLD   How do you know? Maybe it is. You'll never be sure unless you give it a try.

ED   I have tried, Arnold.

ARNOLD   [*Hard*] No you haven't! [*Softer*] You haven't. I wish to God you had, but you haven't.

ED   Arnold, this is not going to do any good for either one of us.

ARNOLD   What makes you so sure of what's good and what's not? Maybe it's just what we need. Maybe it's just what *I* need. You can't expect me to just sit around here waiting for you to call.

ED   I never asked you to. I told you to go out, have a good time, meet other people . . .

ARNOLD   I can't, alright? I'm not built that way.

ED   Well I'm just not ready to make that kind of a commitment.

ARNOLD   I'm not asking you to. But if I have to accept you going out then you have to accept that I'm not.

ED   [*Puzzled*] You really are crazy.

ARNOLD   I'm lonely.

ED   That's not my fault.

ARNOLD   Wanna bet?

ED   You've got no right to make me feel guilty.

ARNOLD   I happen to be in love with you. That must give me some kind of rights. And if that don't give me the right to see you, then at least I got the right to bitch about it. [*Long silence*] You said that you loved me. You do remember telling me that, don't you?

ED   [*Quietly*] Yes.

ARNOLD   Then, do you or don't you?

ED   You know how I feel about you.

ARNOLD   I don't. I wouldn't ask if I did.

ED   Yes. I love you.

ARNOLD   Then what's going on?

ED   What do you want me to say?

ARNOLD   I want you to say what's on your mind. That's what I want. I want you to tell me how in two short weeks we have gone from being lovers to whatever the hell you'd call this?

ED   [*Trying to retain cool*] You are being very difficult.

ARNOLD   [*Mimicking*] You are being very difficult. [*Hard*] Talk to me, goddammit! [*Silence*] Is it your parents coming north? Is that it? Are you ashamed of me?

ED   Of course not.

ARNOLD   Then what?

ED   Not on the phone. What if I come over straight from school tomorrow?

ARNOLD   No! I've got to hear it now. I know what'll happen if you come over, everything will be great just like it always is when we're together and we'll never even mention tonight. No, I want to hear it from this side of you.

ED   [*Checking his watch nervously*] Arnold, I really cannot talk to you now. She'll be here any minute. I'll see you after work tomorrow, O.K.? [*No response*] Arnold? Hello?

ARNOLD   [*Disbelief*] She? Did you say, SHE?

ED   [*Mumbled*] Shit.

ARNOLD   Oh, Shit! Thank God. For a minute I thought you said "She."

ED   I did say she. I am seeing a woman.

ARNOLD   And you called *me* crazy?

ED   Now you know why I didn't want to discuss it on the phone.

ARNOLD   Oh, sure. I can see how much more understandable it would be discussed calmly over a post-sexual cigarette. [*Long pause*] It *is* your parents.

ED   No it isn't!

ARNOLD   Then why all of a sudden like this?

ED   It's not all of a sudden. I just happened to meet her now, that's all. Don't make believe I never told you about my relationships with women.

ARNOLD   Sure you told me about your woman relations. But I thought you meant sisters and aunts and nieces.

ED   That's not funny.

ARNOLD   I think it's hysterical. [*Long pause. He tries to remain calm.*] So, . . . how long has this been going on?

ED   Not long.

ARNOLD   How'd you meet her?

ED   My friends Bob and Janet asked me if I was seeing anyone because they knew this girl they thought I might like to meet.

ARNOLD   And what did you say when they asked if you were seeing anyone?

ED   I said that I wasn't. [*Guilty pause*] Well, I could hardly tell them about you, could I?

ARNOLD   God forbid!

ED   [*Silence. Quietly.*] What are you thinking?

ARNOLD   I am thinking about how it feels to be a no one in the life of someone you love. [*Pause*] Tell me about her.

ED   [*Uneasy*] Why don't you call me a bastard and hang up?

ARNOLD   I want to understand. Talk to me.

ED   I can't . . .

ARNOLD   Please.

ED   Well, she's wonderful.

ARNOLD   Bastard!

ED   You asked!

ARNOLD   I did, didn't I. It's the masochist in me. What'd you tell her about me?

ED   Nothing.

ARNOLD   That does seem to be my name. You did tell her you were bisexual, didn't you?

ED   No. I didn't think it was important.

ARNOLD   Of course not. How silly of me to even mention it.

ED   I'm not so sure that some secrets aren't better kept that way.

ARNOLD   You don't feel that's just slightly dishonest?

ED   No. We have a more mature relationship than that.

ARNOLD   Pardon my naïveté. I didn't know that there really was such a thing as, "Love with the proper stranger." So, when are you taking her to meet your parents?

ED   This weekend.

ARNOLD   I don't believe a word of this. And you're still going to tell me that they have nothing to do with this sudden burst of heterosexuality? [*No response*] Look, Ed, I don't know much about the straight world, but I do know that when a guy takes a gal to meet his folks, for the weekend no less, that this is no casual affair. [*No response*] Don't you feel you're being unfair to lead her on that way? (Not to mention what you're doing to me.) [*No response*] Don't you think she has a right to know what she's letting herself in for? [*No response*] What's the matter? Catch your tongue in the closet door?

ED   You're really dragging me over the coals.

ARNOLD   Why should I be the only one with a barbecued ass? If I may ask another stupid question: What am I supposed to do?

ED   That's up to you.

ARNOLD   Not entirely.

ED   I had hoped that we could go on seeing each other. You may not believe this, but I really don't want to lose you.

ARNOLD   That's hitting below the belt; appealing to my Susan Hayward fantasies. . . . "Arnold, Back Street Woman"!

ED   That's not the way it is at all!

ARNOLD   Then take me to meet your parents.

ED   I could if I wanted to. They'd understand.

ARNOLD   Oh, I know they'd understand. It's you that can't. At least you didn't lie when you said you weren't scared for them to meet me. You're scared they'll meet you!

ED   Thank you very much. Your kindness is appreciated.

ARNOLD   Listen, Mr. Reiss. At this moment I don't think you have a right to expect me to be kind. [*Pulling back*] I'm sorry. I just feel so helpless.

ED   [*Slight relaxing laugh*] You helpless?

ARNOLD   [*Laughing too*] Dumb, huh? [*Cracking*] I don't understand. I thought . . . we were so happy. That we were so special. The way we made love . . . The way you cried in my arms . . . You said you loved me . . .

ED   I do. I always will.

ARNOLD   [*Desperately*] Then what are we doing?

ED   I don't know. I'm confused . . . I'm frightened.

ARNOLD   Ed, come over.

ED   No, I can't. I have made up my mind. I know what I want. I'm doing what I have to do. I know that you are hurting, but that is my decision.

ARNOLD   You can't see what you're doing.

ED   Yes I can. I'm not like you, Arnold. I can't be happy living in a ghetto of gay bars and gay restaurants and backrooms, scared that someone will find out that I'm gay and maybe get me fired. I hate those queens with their bitchy remarks and Bette Davis imitations. I don't want any part of that.

ARNOLD   But that's not us . . .

ED   I want more. I've got to be proud of who I am.

ARNOLD   How can sleeping with a woman make you proud of yourself if you know you'd rather be with a man? How can you ever get any respect from anyone if you won't be yourself? There's no you to respect!

ED   And just where's your self-respect? Huh? I certainly don't see any here!

ARNOLD   You wanna see my self-respect? Here's my self-respect! [*He
          slams down the receiver as the light blacks out on Ed. Then
          . . . calmer.*]
          I fell right into that one.
          [*The lights fade out on Arnold, as the singer is once again
          brought into focus.*]

Scene 4: Arnold

*The bar sounds are heard again as the lights reveal Arnold standing on the
"Stud" platform dressed in denims and swigging from a beer can.*

Look Murray, I am not that lonely! This here's as far as I go. My standards
may lie just left of reactionary, but my limit in a backroom bar is the front
room. Maybe I just better go home, huh? Thank you for taking me out
but . . .

It just ain't my kind of thing, ya' know? I realize you may find this hard to
comprehend, you bein' the way you are, but Murray, I am just not that way
inclined. I mean I'm that way inclined, but I'm not that way inclined. Ya'
know what I mean, Murray? I mean, maybe I'm old fashioned but I like my
sex in a bed. I don't see sex as a spectator sport. I like that one sneaked kiss
in the elevator on the way to a man's apartment. I like the apologies he
makes for the mess the place is in. I dig the dainty tour and arty conversation while he's dimming the lights and pouring the drinks. I like never
finishing those drinks. See Murray, to me a lap in the bed is worth three in a
bar. 'Cause deep down in my heart I know they do not marry sluts. No, they
don't Murray. And it hurts me, Murray, it truly does, to see this multitude
of men so love starved that they resort to sex in a dirty backroom instead of
the way God meant us to be. It is cheap, Murray. And I refuse on moral
grounds to support the degradation these men have brought themselves to.
Period.

Why is it so important to you that I go into that backroom? Are you
a'scared to go in there by yourself? Is that it, Murray? Have I hit on the
nail? C'mon, level it, Murray, are you a'scared?

I am not a'scared, Murray. Oh no I'm not.

Alright, I'll prove it to you. We'll go back there together. But I'm tellin' you
now, I ain't doin' nothin'. O.K.?

O.K. Let's go. [*He starts to turn tentatively and suddenly spins back.*]
Murray, quick, hold my hand. I'm a'scared! What if nobody back there

wants me? It's one thing to go into a regular bar and not get picked up. I mean that happens all the time to lots of people for lots of reasons, but Murray, to go into a place like that and get rejected . . . I don't think I could take it. I know I got personal qualities that put me above and beyond the norm: quick mind, sharp wit, glowing personality. But Murray, what if I don't glow in the dark?

No, I'm O.K. Really. Look, it'll take more than a backroom to set me back. After all, I am an Advocate Experience graduate. Poise, confidence, an open mind . . . they'll never put me away! Lead on.

[*He turns his back to the audience as the lights change to dark red. When he faces front again he is groping to find his way. Loud whisper.*]

Murray? Where are you? Murray? Murray? Oh, there you are. Well, it certainly is dark back here. Hang on a second.

    [*He takes out a book of matches and lights one. He looks around slowly with gaping mouth.*] Oh, my God! [*He blows out the match.*] Murray, quick, let's get outta here. This ain't no place for someone who goes to confessional. I'd jam up the booth for months! [*He freezes. Whisper.*] Murray, Murray? Someone's got his hand on my crotch. What should I do? [*He tries to smile and look natural then he grabs the hand and shakes it.*] Hi there. My name is Arnold, what's yours? Where'd he go, Murray? Oh, Murray, I gotta get outta here. I should've never come.

No I didn't come, Murray! Let's just go, huh? Uh oh. Murray? Someone's got his hand on my heiney. Can you see what he looks like?

Yes it does make a difference, Murray! Murray? Murray? He's reaching around front and opening my belt. Murray? Murray? He's opening my zipper. Murray? Murray? . . . What do I do . . . with the beer can?

    [*He bends over to put the beer can on the ground when he is suddenly penetrated.*]
    MURRAYYYYYYY!!!!!!!
[*At first Arnold's face is twisted in pain and embarrassment as he sways with the humping rhythm. He tries to smile and look comfortable. He feels out the rhythm and quietly enjoys himself for a moment, then he looks unattached, almost bored.*] [*Conversationally*] You come here often? [*The stud hits him on the shoulder.*] No, I don't have to talk. No, that's perfectly alright. I mean, it's not part of my fantasy or anything, conversation that is. Though I must admit I am prone to sweet nothings deftly whispered. However, they are not essential to my enjoyment of the lovemaking experience. I much prefer to open my senses completely to the moment thereby retaining more of an impression whereon to draw on later dates. If you get my drift.

You do? [*He gets hit again.*] But you'd rather I shut up anyway. O.K. I'm not offended. I realize that it must take a lot of concentration for you to keep your . . . concentration in a situation like this so I won't say another word. O.K.? O.K. [*Long pause. He looks around. Adjusts his hands. Then fumbles for a cigarette.*] Cigarette? Oh, I'll save you one for later. Mind if I. . . . That's very understanding of you.

[*He lights a match and tries to light the cigarette but can't because of the motion. He grabs the stud's rear and stops him, lights up then taps him to begin again. Arnold positions his hands in a casual smoker's pose and looks about, puffing deeply.*] Got a nice crowd tonight. Ya' know, this here's easier than I thought it would be. See, I don't usually do this sort of thing, but what with breaking from my lover and all . . . But it's not as bad as I thought it would be. I guess that has a lot to do with you. Your attitude, I mean. I find that being a sensitive person, as I am, that I pick up easily on people's vibrations and hence incorporate them into myself. See, I figured I'd be too uptight to allow for such things. But since you obviously don't care, then I don't care. Just another bar right? Just another night out? Very practical idea. I mean, say you'd picked me up in another bar, well, it might've taken an hour for us to get to this. Or maybe we wouldn't't've gotten along and so never got to find out that we really were so compatible. But this way we can build a relationship the other way around, right? You know, I really like you. Maybe that's a stupid thing to say in a place like this. But if you think about it, it's not so stupid at a time like this, is it? I can't wait to see what you look like.

[*Hit again*] Oh, I'm sorry. I was talking again, wasn't I? Gee, I'm really sorry. It must be my nerves. I guess I'm not as relaxed as I thought 'cause when I get nervous I just talk insistently. On any subject, it don't matter. You just name a subject when I'm nervous and I will talk on and on about it. It don't matter what; sex, drugs, religion, rummage sales, anything. Try it. You'll see. Name a subject. [*The stud pulls out suddenly.*] Oh, you're finished? That was quick. Must'a been hot to trot, huh? [*Miming pulling back on his clothes*] I'd like you to meet this friend of mine. His name is Murray. He must be right around here somewhere. Murray? Murray? Oh, there you are. Murray, I'd like you to meet . . . Hey, I never did catch your naa. . . . [*He split.*] Yoo hoo! Hello? Where'd he go? See, Murray, that's what I've got against places like this. You meet someone nice and you lose him in the dark. I know, I'll light a match. Oh, I don't know what he looks like. Of course, how dumb of me, he's gone out front to wait for me 'cause of the crowd and the smell. C'mon Murray. Let's go find him.

What'd'ya mean, he won't be there? I'm sure he really liked me. He made
love to me, didn't he? Well, didn't he? [*Long pause*] Let's get outta here.

[*Arnold turns his back as the normal bar lights return. He squints and tries to
smile.*] Well, at least I don't have to cook him breakfast. [*Slow fade. Black.*]

Lady Blues sings her final song.

Scene 5

---

*The lights come up on the dressing room set again. They're more general
than before. Ed enters tentatively, looks around, checks his watch and then
sits on the chair at the vanity. He looks at the cards and notes scattered
around the mirror and table. He looks uncomfortable. He checks out the
make-up on the table and picks up a powder puff as Arnold enters. He stops
short in the doorway and stares at Ed who has not heard him come in. There
is a great sadness in Arnold's face. He puts on a huge smile and enters.
Arnold is in a dressing robe.*

ARNOLD   Careful, some of that might rub off on you.

ED   [*Jumping up*] You scared me. [*Holding out his arms*] Hello,
           Arnold.

ARNOLD   [*Walking right past him*] Hello.

ED   Bet you thought you'd never see me again. [*Pause*] You look
           fantastic.

ARNOLD   [*In grand Bette Davis*] Well, aren't you a deah to say so!

ED   The stage manager said it'd be alright for me to wait for you
           in your dressing room. You don't mind, do you? [*No response.
           Arnold sits and begins to peel his face off*] When I asked for
           you as Arnold he didn't know who I meant. [*A little laugh*]
           You look beautiful . . . Really. Lost a little weight, I see.
           [*He reaches out to touch Arnold.*]

ARNOLD   [*Stiffening*] Please . . .

ED   [*Pulling back*] Sorry. I guess you're still pretty angry, huh?

ARNOLD   No, I'm not *still* angry. This is brand new. What are you
           doing here?

ED   I wanted to see you. I've been worried about you. [*Arnold*

	shoots him a look.] I wanted to make sure that you were alright.
ARNOLD	How'd you know I was here?
ED	I saw an ad in the paper.
ARNOLD	That ad should have satisfied your curiosity.
ED	I had planned on seeing the show and just leaving, but when I saw you onstage I had to come back and talk to you. [*Pause*] Been a long time.
ARNOLD	Five months ago you checked out on me with a single phone call. You said that you knew what you wanted and that I wasn't it. I haven't heard a word from you since. What do you want?
ED	Just to see you.
ARNOLD	You've seen me. Get out.
ED	Arnold, please. I'd like to talk to you.
ARNOLD	No.
ED	Wait, just listen to me for a minute.
ARNOLD	NO!
ED	It's got nothing to do with us . . .
ARNOLD	I said no, goddammit! Now just go and leave me alone. [*Softer*] The one nice thing I could say about you was when you left, you left. No matter what I thought of your reasons or lack of them, you kept your word . . .
ED	You knew I'd come back to see you. I told you that I wanted us to be friends. You mean a lot to me. [*Pause. He makes the "I love you" sign and holds it up.*] Arnold? . . .
ARNOLD	Don't get cute with me.
ED	Maybe I shouldn't have come here, but as long as the harm's done can't I talk to you? Just until you're dressed? It's important to me.
ARNOLD	[*Indicating a folding chair against the wall*] Sit down.

ED   [*He gets the chair and sets it behind Arnold.*] So, how you been?

ARNOLD   Can we somehow manage to skip the little niceties and get right to the meat. I know you're here for something.

ED   There is something I have to tell you, but give me a little time. It's not the kind of thing I can blurt right out.

ARNOLD   [*Resigned*] How are your folks?

ED   They're fine. My father had a little trouble with an inner ear infection, but it cleared up nicely.

ARNOLD   They go back south for the winter?

ED   They left two days ago.

ARNOLD   Two days!? What took you so long?

ED   What?

ARNOLD   Ed, you can forget it. It's over. You are not coming back.

ED   You don't understand . . .

ARNOLD   I have never done time in the closet and I sure as hell ain't gettin' in one for you.

ED   But, I don't want to come back. [*Arnold stares.*] Really. Things are going great with Laurel. I tried to tell you. I came to talk to you as a friend. [*Arnold turns back to the mirror. Ed continues merrily.*] We spent a really fantastic summer up-state. We stayed at my parents' place in Florida for a week then back up to the farm. I got a lot done on the house including a new chimney.

ARNOLD   And what'd you do with what's-her-face?

ED   Laurel. Well, at first things were sort of strained. She'd hang around me all the time wanting us to work together. But I talked to her and finally she began doing things on her own. It was hard for her to understand. She doesn't take criticism very well. She tenses up and gets very quiet. Mid-August my sister sent her two kids up for a few days and Laurel took care of them. It was really a marvelous experience for both of us. Sort of like having a family of our own.

ARNOLD   Sounds wonderful! Pa out in the fields, Ma tendin' the young'uns, granma and granpa rockin' on the porch. I'm just sorry you and Laurel couldn't have spent the summer together.

ED   [*Missing that*] You should have seen how Laurel cried when the kids left. But that was nothing compared to the way she carried on when we came back to the city.

ARNOLD   Sounds like she does a lot of crying.

ED   Not so much anymore. We had a talk about that.

ARNOLD   Sounds like you do a lot of talking.

ED   We have a very honest relationship.

ARNOLD   I can see that. You two living together now?

ED   No. We haven't made that kind of a commitment yet. To tell you the truth I'm not sure I could take being with her all the time. She has a way of closing in on me. Actually, it was much easier spending time with you. More relaxed. You're easier to talk to. [*Pause*] I thought about you a lot up there. We would have had a great time.

ARNOLD   I'm not the farm-girl type.

ED   No, you would have loved it. [*Pause*] I worried about you; how you were getting along.

ARNOLD   You could have called and found out.

ED   I thought about it. Once, when everyone was out of the house, I even started dialing.

ARNOLD   What happened?

ED   I didn't think it was fair to build up your hopes.

ARNOLD   [*Dreamily*] There's just one thing I regret about our affair.

ED   [*Sincerely*] What's that?

ARNOLD   That I never beat the shit out of you!

ED   You *are* still angry.

ARNOLD   Where's a tape recorder? No one would ever believe this.

ED   Maybe I'd better go.

ARNOLD   No, please, I'm sorry. Stay, we'll have some wine.

ED   What kind?

ARNOLD   [*Producing a gallon and cups*] House white. Buck-fifty a gallon! You do the honors.

ED   [*Pouring*] Kind'a warm, isn't it?

ARNOLD   [*Taking his cup*] But cooling off nicely. I'm glad you came.

ED   So am I. [*Takes a sip and gags*] God! How do you drink this stuff?

ARNOLD   [*Taking his cup away from him and pouring the wine into his own*] In large doses. So, tell me, how's your sex life?

ED   [*Caught off guard for a moment*] . . . Great.

ARNOLD   [*Sure of himself*] As good as with me?

ED   You're doing it again! Asking questions that you really don't want the answers to.

ARNOLD   Maybe I do.

ED   Arnold, I'm not sure the sex we had was always as good for me as it was for you. Sometimes I felt it got out of control.

ARNOLD   Meaning what?

ED   I don't know. Those last few times, it was like losing myself. I remember once, I don't even think I was conscious. All I remember was kissing you and then nothing until waking in your arms, my body all wet . . .

ARNOLD   And that's bad?

ED   It's not what I want.

ARNOLD   Funny; it's what I pray for.

ED   Well, that's fine when you're twenty-four. But I'm going on thirty-four. I have other needs.

ARNOLD   [*Quietly*] Look at us together in the mirror. Now who would ever believe that you were ten years older than me? I'm aging about as well as a Beach Party movie.

ED   You're beautiful.

ARNOLD   Is *that* why you left?

ED   I didn't leave you because Laurel was prettier.

ARNOLD   I know that. I've seen her. [*Pause*] That morning, after the phone call, I waited in a cab across from your building and watched the two of you leave for work. I was pretty shocked.

ED   We can't all look like Virginia Hamm. I happen to think she's very beautiful.

ARNOLD   Where would you be now if I was a woman?

ED   What?

ARNOLD   If I was a woman. Who would you be with?

ED   But you're not.

ARNOLD   But if I was. Would you ever even have looked at her?

ED   I love her, Arnold.

ARNOLD   Like you loved me?

ED   Like I could never love you.

ARNOLD   Because you never did love me. You were too busy running scared to love me. You were scared I'd leave you. Scared . . . someone would find out about us. Scared . . . you'd let yourself free for once in your life. Oh, I'm vain enough to think you could have loved me, but I don't think you had the time.

ED   [*Quietly*] I did love you. Everything would be very easy for me if I didn't. But I do. [*Long silence*] Sometimes . . . Sometimes when I have trouble reaching orgasm I imagine you behind me just about to . . .

ARNOLD   Does she know? [*Ed shakes his head.*] Have you talked about me at all?

ED   She knows your name. She found one of the drawings you made. The one of the tree outside my dining-room window. She may know more. I saw her looking at that music book you gave me. She didn't say anything, but remember you wrote poems to me on half the pages. [*Long pause*] I couldn't, Arnold. It's not what I want.

ARNOLD   What did you want to tell me? Huh? [*Softly*] You can talk to
           me. I'll understand.

ED   It's nothing really. Just a dream I had last week. I dreamt that
           I was in my parents' house and I went down to my father's
           workshop and got an old rag and a can of turpentine. Then I
           went to the kitchen and got a plastic bag. I took all the stuff
           back up to my bedroom where I soaked the rag in the turpen-
           tine and put it into the plastic bag. Then I got into bed, made
           myself comfortable, pulled the covers right up to my neck
           and then put the plastic bag over my head. The strangest part
           was: as I gathered all the stuff, as I got into bed, as I began
           blacking out from the fumes . . . I was enjoying myself,
           laughing up a storm. [*Break*] The phone woke me in the
           morning. It was Laurel. I couldn't understand what she was
           saying. Half of me was trying to listen to her, the other half
           trying to figure out the dream. I felt dizzy so I went back to
           bed and there, on the pillow, was the plastic bag with the
           turpentine soaked rag. [*Long pause*] I couldn't tell anyone
           else about it. [*Taking Arnold's hand*] This is what I've always
           wanted: you and me together talking. I think I love you more
           now than ever.
           [*Arnold's eyes widen, he jumps up suddenly and begins
           punching Ed wildly. Ed grabs hold of Arnold's arms and
           stretches them out to either side, so that they stand face to face.
           They freeze for a moment searching each other's eyes, then
           suddenly they are in each other's arms, crying, holding each
           other tightly.*]

ED   I'm so scared. I need you.

ARNOLD   [*Gently releasing himself*] O.K. Time out. Everybody back to
           his corner.
           [*Ed sits back down as Arnold crosses to the vanity. Arnold is
           in turmoil. Finally in mock of his opening speech.*]
           Wha' happened!?!
           [*He laughs instead of crying. Crosses behind Ed and tenta-
           tively puts his hands on Ed's shoulders. Ed quickly takes them
           into his. Indecision . . .*]
           You feel better?

ED   [*Happy to be home*] Yes.

ARNOLD   Good. Then get out! [*He grabs back his hands angrily.*] Do you have any idea of what the last five months have been like for me? I cried on so many shoulders . . . I'm sure I lost half my friends. But I always knew you'd be back. But I thought that when you did come back . . . I don't know, that you'd finally have your shit together. And here you are more fucked up than ever. [*Still indecision*] Have you got your car with you? [*Ed nods*] Go get it. I'll . . . I'll get dressed and meet you out front.

ED   Want me to drive you home?

ARNOLD   Huh?

ED   [*Rising*] I'll get the car. [*He exits.*]
            [*Arnold watches him leave then suddenly snaps himself to work. He sits at the vanity and quickly brushes out his hair, clears the table top and begins to undress when just as suddenly he stops and stares at the audience, searching each face.*]

ARNOLD   [*Slowly . . . innocently*] So, what now? Huh? If I take him back now, knowing all I do, maybe I could make it work. With a little understanding? Maybe even a shrink? [*Little laugh*] I *could* just let him drive me home. Then I'd say something like. . . . "The next time you feel you have to say 'I love you' to someone, say it to yourself and see if you believe it!" No, that'd go over his head. I think it went over mine. [*Another little laugh*] Of course I could just leave him waiting out there in the cold. Just slip out the back and really cross him out of my life. That way I'd be over him in a few more months. Give or take a few more friends. I don't know. I don't know. 'Cause if we do start in again, who'd say he won't keep this shit up? Right? I don't know. Maybe that's what I want. Maybe he's treating me just the way I want him to. Maybe I use him to give me that tragic torchsinger status that I admire so in others. If that's true . . . then he's my International Stud. Wouldn't that be a kick in the rubber parts? I love him. That's for sure. [*Fighting back tears*] But do I love him enough? What's enough? This is enough. [*Standing, chin up, confronting the audience*] Enough. [*Slow fade to black*]

THE END

Fugue
in a
Nursery

FUGUE IN A NURSERY premiered at La Mama E.T.C. on February 1, 1979 with the following cast:

LAUREL	*Marilyn Hamlin*
ED	*Edward D. Griffith*
ALAN	*Christopher Marcantel*
ARNOLD	*Harvey Fierstein*

Directed by Eric Concklin
Music by Ada Janik
Stage Design by Bill Stabile
Lighting by Charles Embry
Production Stage Manager: Richard Jakiel
The production was subsequently presented by Mitchell Maxwell at The Orpheum Theatre with Maria Cellario as LAUREL, Will Jeffries as ED and with lighting by Cheryl Thacker.

A NOTE ON THE MUSIC

A full score for Clarinet, French Horn, Violin and Cello was created for the original production by Ada Janik. The music should never overshadow or cause melodramatic effect. Rather it is meant to harmonize the themes and clarify the moments. In Ms. Janik's original score each character was represented by an instrument: Arnold by the Cello, Alan by the Clarinet, Laurel by the Violin and Ed by the French Horn. The musical notations of the text corresponded to the ones of the score.

CHARACTERS
Ed: Thirty-five. Very handsome, masculine with a boyish charm.
Laurel: Thirty-five. Rather unfancy in appearance. Thoughtful and bright though she shows a girlish enthusiasm.
Alan: Eighteen. Shamefully beautiful. A frightened child in hustler's clothing.
Arnold: Twenty-five (going on forty). A kvetch of great wit and want.

TIME
One year after the action of INTERNATIONAL STUD.

PLACE
Arnold's apartment and various rooms of Ed's farmhouse. Only one set is used (see description after prologue).

IMPORTANT
In reading this script it is imperative that close attention be paid to stage directions and character names as the text may become unclear without that information.

Prologue

There will be no pre-show music and the stage should be curtained. (For the La Mama production a revolving stage was used to hide the set from the entering audience.) As the house-lights dim we hear a telephone ringing. During the following conversation (which should be tape-recorded), the audience sees the musicians entering the pit and hears them warming up their instruments. Simultaneously, slides are shown on a screen over the set. We see photos of Arnold in drag, Arnold and Ed walking and talking together, Ed and Laurel in similar leisure pastimes and finally Arnold and Alan together. A telephone rings three times. [A loud radio in the background]

ARNOLD   Happy home for the bewildered.

LAUREL   Hello? Is this Arnold?

ARNOLD   That's what they tell me.

LAUREL   Hi. I don't know where to start. We've never met . . .

ARNOLD   Sounds like my life story. Hang on a second, would you? [*Muffled slightly*] HEY! Could you turn that thing down?

ALAN   [*Far off*] Who is it?

ARNOLD   I don't know but if you'd turn that fakachtah thing down I'd find out!

ALAN   If it's Murray tell him I wanna speak to him. [*The radio noises fade out.*]

ARNOLD   [*Syrupy*] Hello. You still there?

LAUREL   Look, am I interrupting something?

ARNOLD   Nothing you'd wanna write home about. [*Sound of a toilet flushing*] Well, come on. Speak up. I'm a drag queen not a mind reader.

LAUREL   [*Flustered*] Well, like I said, you don't know me but we have a mutual friend. Ed Reiss.

ARNOLD   [*Pause*] Is that what you called to tell me?

LAUREL   No. I'd better start again. You and I have never met. But, I think you'll know who I am. My name's Laurel. Ed and I live together. We're . . . lovers. As you know, Ed has a farm upstate where we spend the weekends and our vacations. Anyway, we got to talking and thought it'd be nice to have you up to visit for a few days. Still with me?

ARNOLD   I'm way ahead of you! I'm sorry but I'm not into any of that kinky stuff.

LAUREL   [*Laughing*] That wasn't our intention at all. I just thought you might like to get out of the city for a few days. Ed's told me so much about you and I've wanted to meet you for the longest time . . .

ARNOLD   Whose idea was this?

LAUREL   We'd both like you to come.

ARNOLD   Yeah, but whose idea was this?

LAUREL   What's the difference? The point is, I know how much Ed values your friendship and that the two of you haven't seen that much of each other lately, which probably has to do with you and I not knowing each other, but hopefully this weekend will straighten all of that out. So, what do you say?

ARNOLD   I don't think so. I appreciate the invite, it was swell of you to call, but I don't think it's such a good idea. But look, maybe after the summer you and I could get together for lunch or something . . .

ALAN   [*Mumbled and muffled*] Wait a minute, I wanna go.

ARNOLD   Hang on a second, would you? [*Muffled conversation*] Listen, Laurel, do you think it'd be alright to bring a friend?

LAUREL   Of course. Please do. I'm sorry I didn't extend an invitation to your friends myself but Ed didn't tell me you were seeing anyone.

ARNOLD   He doesn't know about Alan.

LAUREL   Well, by all means bring him. That'll make the weekend nicer still; to have the both of you. So, we'll pick you up on the Friday train.

ARNOLD   No. We'll be driving up. Alan can borrow a car.

LAUREL   Great. Let me give you the directions.

ARNOLD   That's alright. I think I can remember how to get there.

LAUREL   [*Loaded*] Of course, you've been here before. So, we'll see you Friday. I can hardly wait.

ARNOLD   O.K. See you then.

LAUREL   Bye bye. [*Sound of phones clicking off*]

As the taped conversation ends, a slide appears on the screen:

NURSERY: a fugue

The conductor raises the baton and the first music begins to play. The set is an eight foot by nine foot heavily raked bed. It is mounded with pillows, blankets and all the props needed in the course of the play. It will serve as all rooms in the house. The couples will be lit as separately as possible using color to indicate the pairings when the more complicated conversations begin. Special care should be taken that the four characters never appear to be in bed together. The desired effect is of vulnerability not obscenity.

As the music begins the lights reveal Laurel filing her nails and Ed reading a newspaper. The other couple should not be seen. The music ends. . . .

LAUREL   [*With deep satisfaction*] Isn't this civilized? [*Pause*] Do you think they have enough blankets? Maybe I should . . .

ED   [*Sharply*] They'll be fine.

LAUREL   But it gets awfully cold . . .

ED   [*Final*] Laurel, they'll be fine.

LAUREL   Alright. Don't be so grouchy. [*Cuddling*] Wanna . . . ?

ED   Aren't you tired at all?

LAUREL   I'm too excited about having them here. Don't you wanna . . . ?

ED   Didn't you say you had some paperwork to do?

LAUREL   [*Grabbing away his paper*] You're an old fart you know that.

ED   Where's that newspaper?

LAUREL   [*Handing it back. Bubbling.*] This is just so civilized! Guests up to our country home for the weekend. I can't tell you how excited I am.

ED   We *have* had guests before.

LAUREL   I'd hardly compare this to having your sister and her kids or your parents or even friends from school up. Imagine being hostess to your lover's ex and his new boyfriend. Now if that isn't civilized then what is? It's downright Noel Coward. How's your English accent?

ED   What?

LAUREL   It might be fun to use English accents all weekend.

ED   Would you stop.

LAUREL   What're you being so grouchy about? I'm just fooling around. [*Teasing*] Are my domestic fantasies making you nervous? Don't worry. I promise I won't propose to you.

ED   Very funny.

LAUREL   What is your problem?

ED   I don't see why they can't spend a few quiet days up here without all this rigmarole.

LAUREL   I'm excited. That's all.

ED   . . . Because this is not the weekend that I had planned.

LAUREL   I have no idea what you're talking about.

ED   [*Tossing off the newspaper*] Alan. That's what I'm talking about.

LAUREL   What about him? He seems really nice.

ED   I should've known Arnold would pull something like this.

LAUREL   Now look, I told you that Arnold asked me if he could bring a friend and that I told him he could.

ED   You had no right to. . . . This weekend was supposed to be just the three of us.

LAUREL   So what's the big deal? We've got enough food for four. I didn't have to open another room or anything. What'd you expect Arnold to do? Sit around with us all day then watch us toddle off to bed while he slept alone? It's better this way. You'll see.

ED   No, you'll see. Did you catch the way he fawned over him at dinner? He practically cut his steak for him.

LAUREL   No more than I fawned over you. [*Cuddling*] And I did cut your steak.

ED   [*Pouting*] I could've killed you for that.

LAUREL   You're being ridiculous. There are bound to be compensations on all four of our parts. After all, the two of you were lovers. So little games and jealousies are bound to pop up. But I'm positive it's going to be a great weekend.

ED   Did you see how he made such a point of running off to bed early? "Oh, I'm so tired. All that good food has done me in." His hands all over the boy.

LAUREL   Well, if I had something as pretty as that to go to bed with, I wouldn't stay up late either.

ED   [*Seriously considering*] You think he's pretty?

LAUREL   [*Baiting*] Uh huh.

ED   I don't like them that young.

LAUREL   I do. [*No reaction*] They make a nice couple. Don't you think? [*No answer*] I think Arnold's a very handsome man. Don't know why he'd want to put on a dress.

ED   You really like them that young?

LAUREL   What?

ED   As young as Alan.

LAUREL   [*Considering*] Sure. Why not? All that energy. Did you hear the way their bedsprings were squeaking?

ED   I think I do pretty well in the squeaking department.

LAUREL   [*Teasing*] You do, huh?

ED   [*Moving closer*] Well, making certain allowances for wear and tear . . .

LAUREL   It's too early in the race to make a plea for sympathy.

ED   You want to race? [*Excited*] Alright, we'll race. And may the best man win.

LAUREL   And now, ladies and gentlemen, in the center ring, driving a 1968 Serta Orthopedic . . . couple number 2 . . .

ED   Hey, no tickling before the gun.

LAUREL   On your marks . . . Get set . . . Go!

The lights quickly black out on them and snap on for Alan. He sits straight up in the bed as if frightened out of sleep by a bad dream. A slide appears:

SUBJECT

He takes a deep breath relaxing a bit then looks for Arnold who is hidden under the mountain of blankets. He finds him asleep.

ALAN   [*Shoving his face into Arnold's*] Hello.

ARNOLD   [*Asleep*] If you can't say something nice, don't say nothin' at all. [*He rolls over.*]

ALAN   [*Climbing over to the other side*] Get your fat ass out of bed and get me something to eat. I'm hungry.

ARNOLD   Talk dirty to me.

ALAN   What? . . . Are you asleep?

ARNOLD   [*Opening his eyes wide*] God, you're gorgeous. [*Rolling away*] Now, go away.

ALAN   Come on, wake up.

ARNOLD   But I'm having this flawless dream.

ALAN   About me?

ARNOLD   If it is, will you let me go back to sleep?

ALAN   Yes.

ARNOLD   It's all about you.

ALAN   [*Moving in close*] What about me?

ARNOLD   [*Feeling behind*] My God, you really are awake.

ALAN   That doesn't matter.

ARNOLD   [*Waking more fully*] Maybe not to you . . .

ALAN   Stop changing the subject.

ARNOLD   [*Attacking*] Waste not, want not.

ALAN   Tell me the dream. [*Holding him off*]

ARNOLD   If you like it can we . . . ?

ALAN   No.

ARNOLD   [*Rolling over*] Then I'm going back to sleep.

ALAN   Then I'm going to see if anyone else is up.

ARNOLD   Give my best to the bisexuals.

ALAN   Only he's bisexual. She's straight.

ARNOLD   How do you know?

ALAN   She told me so.

ARNOLD   Too bad. Mixed marriages never work.

ALAN   Yeah, then what were you doing with him?

ARNOLD   Slumming.

ALAN   [*Climbing on top of him*] And what're you doing with me?

ARNOLD   Nothing. It's gone.

ALAN   It'll be back.

ARNOLD   [*Sulking*] But it won't be the same.

ALAN   Of course it will.

ARNOLD   Do you ever think before you speak?

ALAN   No. Do you?

ARNOLD   Frequently. It passes the time while you're speaking.

ALAN   Be nice.

ARNOLD   Go back to sleep and wake up horny.

ALAN   You still haven't told me your dream.

ARNOLD   Why'd you wanna come up here this weekend?

ALAN   What's this black shit on the pillow?

ARNOLD   What black shit on the pillow?

ALAN   This black shit on the pillow.

ARNOLD   It's black shit on the pillow.

ALAN   Bullshit.

ARNOLD   Bull shit, black shit, why'd you wanna come?

ALAN   What do you mean?

ARNOLD   Never mind. Talk dirty to me.

ALAN   Tell me the dream.

ARNOLD   I ain't tellin' you nothin'. You lied to me.

ALAN   About what?

ARNOLD   You said it would come back. What's it waiting for?

ALAN   It's waiting to hear the dream.

ARNOLD   [*Peeking under the covers*] Is it really into that sort of stuff?

ALAN   We're waiting.

ARNOLD   How old are you?

ALAN   You know how old I am.

ARNOLD   Tell me again, I need reassurance.

ALAN   The dream?

ARNOLD   I know who you are. You're the son I always avoided having. Why's the lamp on?

ALAN   It's still dark out.

ARNOLD   Is there a storm?

ALAN   No, the sun's not up yet.

ARNOLD   You woke me in the middle of the night again?

ALAN   Do you mind?

ARNOLD   Of course not. [*Taking the boy into his arms like a child*] Come on. What frightened you?

ALAN   Nothing. I just felt like talking.

ARNOLD   Comfortable?

ALAN   Tighter. Did Ed ever have bad dreams?

ARNOLD   Everyone does.

ALAN   Did you have to hold him?

ARNOLD   Talk dirty to me.

ALAN   Get me a dog.

ARNOLD   Why?

ALAN   I want one.

ARNOLD   I don't give you things.

ALAN   Yes you do. [*Arnold stiffens.*] No you don't. But, a dog's not a thing.

ARNOLD   All the more reason.

ALAN   C'mon, get me a dog.

ARNOLD   I have no money for a dog.

ALAN   You can get one at the pound. They're free.

ARNOLD   Then get one yourself.

ALAN   I will. Can I keep it at your place?

ARNOLD   You shouldn't wear cologne. It tastes terrible.

ALAN   Sometimes they have dogs up for adoption in the paper. Where's that other copy of the *Voice?*

ARNOLD   Under the bed. [*Alan starts for it.*] No, don't move. I want to remember me like this forever.

ALAN   I want a cigarette anyway.

ARNOLD   [*Sulking*] Is that what you tell the other models at the studio; that I buy you things and that's why you live with me?

ALAN   No. Of course not.

ARNOLD   You make more money modeling for an hour than I do in a week. I don't buy you things. Don't say I do.

ALAN   I don't.

ARNOLD   Good. 'Cause I don't. Not things. Cigarettes. That's all.

ALAN   Alright already. Want a cigarette?

ARNOLD   They're mine, aren't they?

ALAN   Then do you mind if I have one?

ARNOLD   That's why they're here. Don't do that to yourself; treat yourself like a piece of meat. It's what all them leering faggots do, so you don't have to do it to yourself.

ALAN   [*Lighting a cigarette*] I don't.

ARNOLD   At least stop enjoying it. You don't have to be a model.

ALAN   You don't have to be a drag queen.

ARNOLD   How ridiculous! They're not the same things at all.

ALAN   What's the difference?

ARNOLD   A model IS. A drag queen . . . Aspires.

ALAN   Great aspirations!

ARNOLD   Very funny. I'm serious, Alan. Fantasies are fine in the bedroom, but outside they're not fantasies, they're lies.

ALAN   What are you talking about?

ARNOLD   Your hustler trips.

ALAN   [*Stuffs cigarette in Arnold's mouth*] Would you stop? Where's that newspaper?

ARNOLD   [*Handing it over*] Here.

ALAN   [*Long look at Arnold*] I love you.

[*Arnold rolls into Alan's arms as the lights fade down on them and up on Laurel and Ed. They are in each other's arms.*]

LAUREL   I don't believe I've seen you this turned on in months. If that's Arnold's effect on you then I think I'll ask him to move in.

ED   It's not Arnold, it's you.

LAUREL   Is that why you called me Arnold?

ED   I did not.

LAUREL   [*Giggling*] Oh yes you did. Deep into loving you whispered
            into my ear, "I love you, Arnold."

ED   That's not funny. You shouldn't make up things like that.

LAUREL   I'm not. What're you getting so upset about? Minds wander
            during sex. It's like dreaming; all sorts of things pass through
            the mind. I once blurted out the phone number of the house
            I grew up in. I'm not upset you called me Arnold, so there's
            no reason for you to be.

ED   I never called you Arnold. That's something passing in *your*
            mind.

LAUREL   Alright. So I misheard you. Take it easy.

ED   It's that damned kid. This was going to be a beautiful week-
            end. The three of us together. I thought . . . that having
            the two of you here together . . . that I'd be able to put a
            period on that whole section of my life. But the second he
            walked through the door I knew that I'd put the period there
            long ago and this whole weekend was unnecessary.

LAUREL   Well, thanks a lot. I'm glad you've made up your mind.

ED   That's not what I meant. I wasn't planning on comparing the
            two of you. Christ! Everything was going to be so simple, I
            wanted us all to be friends. Then Arnold had to bring that
            kid.

LAUREL   He also brought a cake, a lace tablecloth and the *Village
            Voice*. [*Handing him the paper*] Enjoy them all.

ED   [*Trying to cuddle*] Come here and I'll read you the funny
            pages.

LAUREL   I have my own reading, thank you.

[*She picks up some papers as the lights cross back to Arnold and Alan in
each other's arms.*]

ARNOLD   Feels so strange. I can't get over it; you and I in this room
            with them in there. This was my room, y'know. I mean, we
            slept together in there but I kept my clothes in here in case
            any neighbors or family dropped in and peeked around. He
            didn't want them to think we were queer or anything. I can't
            believe I put up with that.

ALAN   So, what do you think?

ARNOLD About what?

ALAN   Ed. Seeing him again with me to compare him to.

ARNOLD Is that what I'm supposed to be doing?

ALAN   Sure. I have.

ARNOLD So, what do you think?

ALAN   He ain't so hot. Not hot enough to be "The Great Love of Your Life" anyway.

ARNOLD I don't consider him "The Great Love of My Life." But, he's got his good points. He's good natured, good looking, good in bed . . .

ALAN   . . . Good and boring.

ARNOLD He's not good and boring. He's just plain boring. But there's worse things to be. I once knew this guy who . . .

ALAN   There's a lot of that going around.

ARNOLD Hey, who's the straight-man here?

ALAN   I'm at that impressionable age. You're rubbing off on me.

ARNOLD [*Blanche du Bois*] I never touched the Gray boy.

ALAN   [*Laughs*] Feel better?

ARNOLD Yeah. So anyway, I once knew this guy . . .

ALAN   Did you really love Ed?

ARNOLD I guess so.

ALAN   And he loved you.

ARNOLD I wouldn't say that.

ALAN   I would. I see how he looks at you. Why'd you two break up?

ARNOLD We wanted different things.

ALAN   Like what?

ARNOLD I wanted a husband and he wanted a wife.

ALAN   You ever think of going back with him?

ARNOLD   You can't go back.

ALAN   Why not?

ARNOLD   Because.

ALAN   Because why?

ARNOLD   Because . . . because . . . because people change. They're
          never the same twice. So how can you go back?

ALAN   Well, did you ever want to start out fresh again?

ARNOLD   Jesus Christ! Were you ever not true to form? Thank God I
          was not your mother. I could have denied you nothing. I am
          in awe of her that she denied you as much as she did for you
          to need to ask for so much now.

ALAN   When I said that I loved you before, you didn't answer me.

ARNOLD   I didn't realize that it was a question.

ALAN   Well?

ARNOLD   Here, read the newspaper. [*Throws it at him*] [*Alan rolls
          away*] Are you pouting? This child is unbelievable. Come, I'll
          read to you. O.K.? O.K.

A slide appears on the screen:

CODETTA

*The lights come up on Laurel and Ed reading the paper in the same position
as the other couple. Both couples are visible but the separation is clear.*

ED   [*Reading from the paper*] Banes, Iowa. "That'll teach them
          folks not to mess around with true love," beamed eighty year
          old Sarah Fonedwell as she left the Iowa courtroom arm in
          arm with her fifteen year old boyfriend.

          Miss Fonedwell was charged with statutory rape and
          impairing the morals of a minor after the young boy's parents
          learned that their son was having intimate relations with the
          great-grandmother of six. The couple had met when the boy
          took over a friend's paper route. Miss Fonedwell was a steady
          customer. Judge John Sirrocco dismissed the charges saying,
          "No real harm was done. It's all in the boy's education." But
          before adjourning court he shook a warning finger at the
          feisty lady saying, "From now on you'd better walk to the

corner when you want a paper." To which she quipped, "I don't mind the added exercise, but I sure will miss them home deliveries." [*The couples keep the integrity of their pairing while building in rhythm.*]

LAUREL   You made me stop working to listen to that?

ED   I think it's very funny. Don't you?

ARNOLD   That's disgusting.

LAUREL   Would you think it was so funny if it had been an eighty year old man seducing a fifteen year old girl? You think the judge would have said it was all in her education?

ED   But it wasn't.

ALAN   I don't know, I think it's kind of sexy.

LAUREL   Sexy?

ED   Yeah, sure. Imagine his feeling of power. The strength he must have felt: he young and virile, she old and withered drinking in his youth . . .

ALAN   Think of the pleasure he gave her. I bet she even thought she was fifteen again.

LAUREL   You see him as the giver and her as the taker? That's even more perverse than I'd imagined it. I saw her giving her last favor; passing on her last gift to the next generation. But you see it as a simple matter of lust.

ED   Well if you'd listened to the way she talked, you'd see she's obviously just a dirty old lady.

ARNOLD   I can't believe that anyone would be that self destructive. I mean, if she was eighty to begin with, how old was she when it was over?

ALAN   Obviously, she was rejuvenated in his arms. A miracle of modern sex.

ARNOLD   The only miraculous thing about modern sex is that it exists.

LAUREL   Did you ever sleep with someone then wonder who gave more; or who enjoyed it more?

ARNOLD   Could we change the subject?

ALAN   [*Pushing Arnold away*] They don't buy the milk if they can
            get the cow for free.

ARNOLD   That's what I like to hear: Good old American "not now."

LAUREL   At the risk of rendering you impotent for the remainder of
            "The Milkman's Matinee," could you make love to me if I
            was an eighty year old woman and you a fifteen year old boy?

ALAN   Fierce, passionate love.

ARNOLD   Ah, but would I make love to you?

ED   Why not?

LAUREL   You could really sleep with an eighty year old woman?

ED   Are we talking about me or me if I was fifteen?

ALAN   At least she was willing to give it a go.

ED   I give what I can and trust that it's enough.

ALAN   Not unless you can slip in a few one liners.

ED   I don't lie awake nights wondering whether I gave more or
            you gave more or about how old you are or if you're pretty or
            not. And yes I could probably make love to an eighty year old
            woman. I could make love to an eighty year old camel. I could
            probably make love to anything . . . as long as it kept its
            mouth shut.

[*The lights go out on Laurel and Ed.*]

ALAN   Ssssshhh! [*Listening*] I thought I heard someone talking.

ARNOLD   It was probably Ed talking in his sleep.

ALAN   He talks in his sleep?

ARNOLD   Talks, screams, gnashes his teeth, kicks . . .

ALAN   Really? How'd you ever get any sleep?

ARNOLD   I never slept better.

ALAN   You really loved him, huh?

ARNOLD   We starting that again?

ALAN   I'm just curious. Why?

ARNOLD   What'd'ya mean, "Why?" Why does anyone love anyone?
          Because I did. Because . . . I did. Because . . . he let me.

A slide appears on the screen:

STRETTO

*Alan appears alone in a light as Arnold and Ed prepare for the scene. During
this section both Alan and Laurel will appear in their own lights regardless to
whom they speak. Arnold and Ed will appear center stage together.*

ALAN   I'm not talking to you. Deserting me all afternoon like that.
          Where the hell did the two of you disappear to anyway?

ARNOLD   We spent the afternoon in bed. Jealous?

ALAN   Why should I be? You didn't do anything.

ARNOLD   How do you know? We were alone for three hours.

LAUREL   If you say you only talked then I believe you. Though I can't
          say I understand why you had to do it in bed.

ARNOLD   You remember that poem about sleep: That in sleep all men
          are equal, the pauper and the king and all that?

ED   Something about there being no limitations on dreams?

ARNOLD   Yeah, that's the one. Well, I figure if everyone's equal in sleep
          then just lying down makes you at least reachable. Besides,
          that's where I do my best thinking. Don't have to worry
          about the body, it just relaxes leaving all the blood for the
          brain.

ED   I used to call your bedroom the Nursery, remember? It was
          always so warm and comfortable and safe.

ARNOLD   I thought it was because we never went to bed without a
          bottle.

ED   And you saved every bottle we drank together. You still have
          them?

ARNOLD   Nah.

ED   You said you wanted to make something out of them.

ARNOLD   When we broke up I did. Quite a racket. [*Mimes throwing
          bottles*] And quite a mess. So tell me, what's new with you?

ED   Not much.

ARNOLD   Well, are you seeing anyone? [*Ed laughs*] That wasn't sup-
                posed to be funny. You have been known to sidestep on
                occasion.

ED   Not since we've been together.

ARNOLD   Give it time.

ED   I doubt it. I really do love her very much.

ARNOLD   I'm happy for you. What can I say? It's what you said you
                wanted and I'm glad it's working out.

ED   Are you jealous?

ARNOLD   No. Should I be?

ED   You don't love him.

ARNOLD   What's that got to do with anything?

ED   'Cause I'm jealous of him anyway.

LAUREL   [*To Alan*] So, tell me about yourself.

ALAN   [*To Arnold*] I had to talk to her all afternoon. Nothing else to
                do with the two of you running off. Y'know she tried to make
                me? It's the truth. And not even me. I mean it wasn't me she
                was trying to make, particularly. She's just got this thing for
                faggots. It's true. Ask her. She'll tell you the whole story. I
                think she likes to tell the story as much as she likes to make
                the faggots. Anyway, she's proved you wrong. You said people
                only went after me because of my looks, but she went after
                me because of my likes.

ED   [*With Arnold in his arms*] This feels wonderful.

ALAN   You know, at first I was insulted; being wanted just because
                I'm gay. But, that's almost like being wanted for myself . . .
                I think I'm flattered.

ARNOLD   [*To Ed*] Hey, watch your hands. I'm a married man.

LAUREL   [*To Alan. They are now lit together.*] So, tell me about your-
                self.

ALAN   I'm a model. Clothes, toothpaste . . . anything they can
                sell with an All-American puss. I'd like to be an actor, but I

think I'll let that ride until I've made all I can out of being the American Dream.

LAUREL   And what about your childhood?

ALAN   According to Arnold, it's only just begun.

LAUREL   Arnold really is something else. You two must be very happy together.

ALAN   Believe me, there are easier things than living with Arnold. He thinks it's immoral, that it makes him a lesser person to love me because I'm good-looking.

LAUREL   Oh come on.

ALAN   No, really. He'd be much happier if I was his age, his size, his . . . size. Sometimes I'm not sure if he wants a lover or a bookend.

LAUREL   It's good that you have a sense of humor. Ed has none. But that's part of his charm.

ALAN   No wonder they didn't last.

LAUREL   Well, I think there's more to it than that. But I can't tell you how happy I am that Arnold has you. My reasons may be a little selfish. Y'know, they were still going together when I met Ed. I didn't know it of course. If I did I never would have started seeing Ed. See, I met him through a friend from group . . .

ALAN   Group? Like in therapy group?

LAUREL   That's right. It's kind of a story, I guess. I had just come through a rather bad affair with a guy who turned out to be bisexual. (The bi leaning toward his new boyfriend.) When he broke the news to me I was quite a mess. See, he wasn't the first man to pull that on me. All told there were three of that particular persuasion plus a pair of married men thrown in for good measure. Not the greatest track record for a "One Man Woman" type like myself. I became what you could call . . . depressed. And when I looked among my friends for a sympathetic ear I realized that every one of them was gay. That's when it began to dawn on me that I might just have gotten myself into a rut. So, off to therapy I went. That's where I met Janet who told me about a handsomely available teacher she knew named Ed. She set up the get together and that was that.

ALAN   A real live blind date. How exotic.

LAUREL   [*Amused*] Blind indeed. We'd been dating for over a month before he ever told me about Arnold. But by then, it was too late to pull out without a fight.

ALAN   So you fought?

LAUREL   No, that's not what I meant. I mean, it wasn't a fight. I just pulled back enough to let Ed feel his freedom: No promises, no pressure, no commitments. Soon he was telling me that he wanted to end his relationship with Arnold. So, I suggested he speak to my therapist and he joined the group . . .

ARNOLD   You never told me about the shrink.

ED   Because I know how you feel about "Shrinks." But really, the group's been very supportive. They've never pushed me toward any decision that I didn't want to make.

ARNOLD   Now I know where all that, "I owe myself the chance to lead a normal life" bullshit came from. So, I suppose you're straight now?

ED   Not now. I always have been.

ARNOLD   And me? . . . and all the others, what were we; a phase you were going through?

ED   [*Laughing*] You always were a homosexual chauvinist. To you everyone's either gay or in the closet.

ARNOLD   What's sex like with her?

ED   It's very beautiful.

ARNOLD   Is it satisfying?

ED   I'm with her, aren't I?

ARNOLD   So, what does that mean? I could've kept you. You don't believe it, but it's true. I've done a lot of thinking about you and some of the others I've been through and I think I've found a pattern: When things get too good . . . I get out. Well, I guess to a degree we all do. But most pull out; ride off into the sunset with a wave and a wink and a "Heigh-o-

Silver." But not me. I am a pusher. I nudge and kvetch and cry and demand until I leave my partner no possible alternative but for him to run for his life. That makes him the villain and leaves the victim role to me. And "Poor Pearl" is a role I really love to play.

ED   I never saw myself the villain.

ARNOLD   You never saw yourself period.

ED   I wouldn't have stayed. In the year that Laurel and I have been seeing each other I haven't once fooled around. And believe me, our relationship allows for that. No, I wouldn't have stayed. [*Thinks*] I bet you think you could get me back if you wanted to.

ARNOLD   I don't want to. That's precisely my point. Why waste all that energy? When an affair hits the skids you shed it like last year's fashion and head back to the streets. There are plenty more where that one came from. And that, my ex-husband, is what I call the miracle of modern sex.

LAUREL   We attend private sessions on Tuesdays and on Thursdays we have group. You and Arnold should try it. Maybe not the private sessions but a group's the ideal way to open up the lines of communication between two people and really solidify a relationship.

ALAN   Sounds inspiring.

ED   And what about you? You don't love that kid.

ARNOLD   You said that, not me.

ED   So, do you?

ARNOLD   Maybe. What makes you think I'm in love with anyone?

ED   Because we've been lying in bed together for over an hour in and out of each other's arms and you've yet to make a pass at me.

ARNOLD   That's not love. That's good taste.

ED   Come on, Arnold, who is it? No, let me guess . . . Could it be me?

ARNOLD   [*Jumping*] God, the EGO!!!!

ED   [*Pulling him back*] I was only kidding.

ARNOLD   You wouldn't know him anyway. I don't know him. Not
            really.

ED   You wouldn't love him if you did.

ARNOLD   You're really impossible.

ED   [*Genuine*] Who is he?

ARNOLD   Well, you know The International Stud Bar has this dark
            backroom where everyone goes to fool around . . . What
            am I telling you for? I wouldn't know about such things if it
            wasn't for you showing them to me. Anyway, I've been going
            there a lot lately. Two, three times a week.

ED   What does Alan have to say about that?

ARNOLD   [*Sarcastically*] We have a very honest and open relationship.
            So, there's this guy there that I meet every night and we
            always get it on together. We haven't talked about anything
            really and we meet there only by chance, I mean we haven't
            set it up that way or anything. It's just that he's always there
            waiting for me, or if I get there first I wait for him . . . Oh,
            never mind.

ED   No, go on, it sounds very romantic.

ARNOLD   Just forget it, alright?

ED   I'm sorry, but first you tell me you're in love. Then you tell me
            you can only get it on in a backroom . . .

ARNOLD   That's not it at all.

ED   Have you ever made love together alone?

ARNOLD   No, but . . .

ED   Have you ever had a drink together in the light of the front
            room?

ARNOLD   He's very shy.

ED   [*Laughing*] Arnold, I think you've reached a new plateau of
            perversity.

ARNOLD   Hey, wait a minute here, who gospelled to whom about the advantages of the backroom? I'd never seen a backroom until after you. . . .

ED   I never took you into one.

ARNOLD   But that's where you would rather have taken me. If we'd met and stayed in the backroom we never would have had the problems we did.

ED   Is that your answer now? Put the blame on me. "Ed, you hurt me so bad. I'll never trust to love again." So, you're going to play this one nice and safe.

ARNOLD   Look who's knocking safety! Mr. All-American Heterosexual! Locked your life up tight didn't you. Picked yourself a nice little wifey type, plain and lonely enough to never worry about her stepping out on you, pleasant and giving enough to boss her around to get her to do anything or go anywhere that you want. And you're gonna read my beads?[*Arnold makes a dive under the covers.*]

ED   Hey! What are you doing?

ARNOLD   [*Emerging at the foot of the bed next to Ed's feet, his feet next to Ed's face*] Take it easy. I'm just looking for a second opinion.

ED   I thought you were trying to get to the bottom of me.

ARNOLD   Heterosexuality has done "nada" for your wit. Your feet stink.

ED   They weren't expecting company.

ARNOLD   [*Picking up a bottle*] What's this?

ED   My cologne.

ARNOLD   [*Sniffing*] What is it, "Ben Hur"? [*Sprinkles it about*] Now I'm in my element. Toss me a pillow. [*Ed does*] Thanks. And just what's wrong with playing it safe? I can sleep when I want, eat when I want, fuck when I want . . .

ED   . . . Want when you want.

ARNOLD   Cheap shot.

ED   Can I just ask you a question? If you don't love Alan, why do you stay with him?

ARNOLD   He needs me.

ED   Come on.

ARNOLD   Alright, I need him.

ED   Forget I asked.

ARNOLD   What the hell would you know about need? You're like a baby
         in a crib, hands and fingers flexing, "Gimme. Gimme."
         You're all want. So, maybe I don't love him, but I need that
         gorgeous imbecile and I like to think that he needs me.

ED   So, he's like a pet.

ARNOLD   You're a pig, you know that?

ED   Arnold, I am exhausted from trying to understand.

ARNOLD   It gets easier with practice. He ain't complaining.

ED   Don't you think he deserves to be loved?

ARNOLD   Of course he does. Who doesn't? But, who is?

ED   I am.

ARNOLD   What do you suppose it is that makes me want to shove a
         chair up your nose? [*Pause*] What the hell am I supposed to
         do: sit around crying over losing you?

ED   That's not what I meant. I'm very happy you have him,
         alright?

ARNOLD   [*Long pause*] You and Laurel working on having kids yet?

ED   We haven't really discussed it in detail.

ARNOLD   Don't you still want kids?

ED   Still? Who said anything about having kids?

ARNOLD   You did. Don't you remember?: At the party there was that
         woman who arranged for gay couples to adopt. You probably
         don't remember, you said you wanted a boy, but you were gay
         then.

ED   I remember. But that was just talk. You know, a fantasy.

ARNOLD   Is that what it was?

ED   Sure, like our airplane, and our island . . .

ARNOLD   . . . and our relationship.

ED   That was one of the things that made me love you: that I
         could fantasize about anything, let my mind go as far out as it
         could and there you were all caught up in the dream with me,
         making it almost real.

ARNOLD   'Cause I didn't know it wasn't. Those things weren't fantasies
         to me. To me a fantasy is a Genie or a magic lamp, something
         impossible that you wouldn't really want even if you could
         have it. Our airplane, our island, our child . . . they weren't
         fantasies. They were possibilities. None of it was impossible.
         Y'know, I keep a ledger where I list things like that. And
         when I get an item that's on the list I put a checkmark next to
         it. The ledger's got more than one hundred pages filled with
         my possibilities. You'd be surprised how many checkmarks
         there are too. Oh, they're little things like an electric tooth-
         brush, or an azalea bush or a subscription to *National Geo-
         graphic*. But they each mark an achievement for me.

ED   What's the inflation ratio; items as opposed to checkmarks?

ARNOLD   Never counted.

ED   Am I on the list?

ARNOLD   Listed and checked off.

ED   That's cheating. You don't have me.

ARNOLD   [*Cocksure*] Don't I?

ED   No.

ARNOLD   I'll be sure to correct my ledger first thing Monday morning.

ED   [*Pause*] Tell me something, what would you do with a sub-
         scription to *National Geographic*?

ARNOLD   [*Hiding his insult*] Look at the dirty pictures.

ED   [*Agreeing*] Oh.

Arnold pulls a pillow over his head in disgust as a slide appears on the screen:

COUNTER SUBJECT

*Arnold and Alan are in each other's arms just waking. The other two remain
in the dark until indicated.*

LAUREL   [*Calling out*] Hurry up, you two sleepyheads, breakfast is on the table.

ARNOLD   Sleepyheads?

ALAN   [*Ecstatic*] Breakfast? How'd you sleep?

ARNOLD   Awfully. I dreamt that I was walking down this twisting path and no matter how carefully I watched I kept stepping in cowpies . . .

ALAN   You mean cow-chips. Not pies. Chips.

ARNOLD   Whatever. Anyway, as I turned a corner around this big Camperdown Elm I saw Ed squatting down naked making the cowpies . . . or chips. Now what the hell do you suppose that was supposed to mean?

ALAN   Maybe it was prophetic dreaming.

ARNOLD   Prophesying what?

ALAN   Maybe the toilet's gonna bust.

LAUREL   [*Calling out*] C'mon you two. We'll be late for church.

ARNOLD   She say church?

ALAN   Didn't you know, Ed plays organ for the services every Sunday morning.

ARNOLD   Give me a break. And they say dreams are meaningless?

LAUREL   [*Now lit*] Aren't you two coming?

ARNOLD   Actually, Laurel, I'd love to go but my religion strictly forbids entering any church for other than historical purposes; looking at stained glass etc.

LAUREL   Nonsense. I have lots of Jewish friends that visit churches.

ARNOLD   Oh, but I'm not Jewish anymore. I've converted. I'm what you'd call a Scientific American. Yes. See . . . we believe that all of mankind's problems can be solved with vitamins.

ALAN   [*Under his breath*] Groan!

LAUREL   So, you have no need for prayer.

ARNOLD   I wouldn't say that. I'm often found on my knees.

ALAN   [*A bit louder*] Groan!

LAUREL   But if you can't enter a house of God, where do you pray?

ARNOLD   Harvard.

ALAN   [*Loud*] Groan!!! [*Arnold leaps on him laughing.*]

ED   [*Lights on him and Laurel*] What's the matter?

LAUREL   Nothing. Are you ready?

ED   Are they coming down?

LAUREL   No. They're sleeping in.

ED   What's the matter? Did Arnold say something?

LAUREL   I'm not upset. Are you coming?

ED   This weekend's not turning out the way you thought it would either. Is it? Just remember, it was your idea.

LAUREL   I like Arnold. I really do. It's just . . . When I thought about this weekend I knew it was a set-up for all sorts of competitions, comparisons . . . and I was ready for them. After all, I knew no matter what happened that I had you. I knew you'd made your choice between us and felt I could deal with anything knowing you had chosen me.

ED   That's what I've been saying all along.

LAUREL   Would you just listen? . . . That's not what's happening here. Arnold is so relaxed, as if he has nothing on his mind, like he's simply visiting friends for the weekend.

ED   What's wrong with that?

LAUREL   He's just too sure of himself. Like a kid all puffed up with a secret.

ED   Are you sorry they're here?

LAUREL   No. Just aware. [*Lights out on them*]

ALAN   You weren't very nice to her.

ARNOLD   I do have my limits and one of them happens to be Sunday morning Mountain Church services. Actually, I'm shocked that Ed let her ask us at all. He probably would have introduced us as long lost relatives. The charcoal-grey sheep of the family.

ALAN   Kissing cousins. So, what do you make of her?

ARNOLD   She's alright. A little too giving and gracious for my tastes, but deep down she's a survivor.

ALAN   How can you say that? She makes the same mistakes over and over.

ARNOLD   Once is a mistake. Twice a misfortunate coincidence. But three times and you can start writing your memoirs.

ALAN   He's number four.

ARNOLD   I wonder if maybe she's really gay? I know just the woman to bring her out too. Bet she'd make a great lesbian.

ALAN   And you'd make a great lamp.

ARNOLD   I'm afraid I'd make a great deal more than that.

ALAN   [*Climbing onto him*] I'll make do . . .

Lights out on them as a slide appears on the screen:

STRETTO

Lights come up on all four holding plates and napkins as if they've just finished lunch. They begin to pass the plates to Laurel.

ED   Laurel, that was a delicious lunch. Isn't she a great cook, Arnold? Besides being beautiful.

ARNOLD   [*Snatching the pile of plates from Laurel*] Just delicious. And beautiful.

ALAN   I bet I've gained five pounds in the past two days.

ARNOLD   Here, let me help you with those dishes.

LAUREL   [*Grabbing the dishes back.*] No, I'm fine. Ed, why don't you take Arnold and Alan out to the barn and show them our new canning machine. We've been canning all our own vegetables, you know.

ARNOLD   Really? Ed, why don't you take Alan and show it to him. He's the real can connoisseur in the family. I'll stay and help

Laurel. We've yet to have a moment alone to compare notes on you.

ED   Just what Laurel's been waiting for.

LAUREL   [*Embarrassed*] Ed!

ED   [*Taking two glasses*] Let's hit the road before the fur starts flying. Grab that bottle of brandy. No need for us to rough it. [*There is a sudden light change focusing on Arnold and Alan in the center of the bed. Ed moves to the upstage right corner of the bed as Laurel moves with her dishes and dishrag to the downstage left corner. When Ed speaks it is to Alan's next physical position.*]

ALAN   Go start packing. We're getting out of here tonight.

ARNOLD   Would you stop.

ALAN   I suppose you're going to tell me you spent another innocent afternoon in bed. Only this time with her.

ARNOLD   It was not an afternoon, it was only an hour. And we spent it in the kitchen doing dishes. You knew where we were. If you were lonely you should have come in.

ALAN   Oh, I wasn't lonely. I had lots of company. He tried to make me.

ARNOLD   Would you please . . .

ALAN   I'd like to be able to spend two minutes in this house without someone trying to shove me onto a couch . . .

ED   Would you like another brandy?

ALAN   . . . And you put down the studio? At least when someone makes a pass at me there it's got a trip to Europe or a movie contract as part of the deal. Here it's "Alone at last!" and a dive for my zipper.

ED   Well, here we are: Alone at last.

ARNOLD   Alan, when we walk down the street and an old lady asks you for the time you swear she's trying to make you. Now I'd be the last to say you weren't irresistible, but, Angel, there are limits. [*Joins Laurel*]

ED   We can sit on this haystack. [*Alan joins him.*]

ARNOLD   [*Wiping a dish*] Isn't this civilized? Doing the dishes.

LAUREL   Stuck with the dishes. I feel like we went out to lunch, you thinking that I was treating and I thinking that you were treating and here we are: working off the bill.

ARNOLD   No, I know, we're in-laws on one of them detergent commercials.

LAUREL   "Why Marge, your dishes are so shiny. I can see myself!"

ARNOLD   "Well, so can I!" Platter, platter on the stack. Does she think I want him back? [*He winces a bit.*]

LAUREL   You work fast. I thought we'd kind'a waltz around the table a few times first.

ARNOLD   Sorry, I thought we might as well get it out of the way.

LAUREL   So, do you?

ARNOLD   What do you think?

LAUREL   I think you do.

ARNOLD   Really. Why?

LAUREL   Well, you don't love Alan.

ARNOLD   I keep hearing that. What makes you think I don't love Alan?

LAUREL   How could you when you still love Ed?

ARNOLD   What makes you think I still love Ed?

LAUREL   Well, I know that from the start you loved Ed more than he loved you . . .

ARNOLD   He told you that?

LAUREL   It's nothing to be ashamed of.

ARNOLD   Of course not. If it's true that one person always loves more than the other, why not be the one who feels the most? But why would that make you think I'd want him back now?

LAUREL   You're here, aren't you?

ARNOLD   You asked me to come.

LAUREL   Still, you didn't have to. [*Uncomfortably*] Look, I know more about your relationship than you might think. We have few secrets and a great deal of openness. It's the kind of relationship we have. We share almost everything with complete freedom . . . What I'm trying to say is that I know a great deal of what was said between you . . .

ARNOLD   So?

LAUREL   Please. So, I know what it feels like to be in that position. You felt hurt, rejected, angry . . . Then you started to wonder if there was ever anything between you. Or maybe you'd made it all up? Who's to blame for that? Who's to blame for breaking up?

ARNOLD   Are we talking about you or me?

LAUREL   You told Ed that you could get him back if you wanted to.

ARNOLD   I also told him that I didn't want to.

LAUREL   Then why do you call him all the time? I know about your calls in the afternoon while I'm at work.

ARNOLD   He told you that I call him?

LAUREL   [*Haughty*] I told you, we have a very honest relationship.

ARNOLD   Laurel, I don't want you to misunderstand and think I'm calling Ed a liar, but I've never called him. Yes, we've spoken on the phone, but he has always called me. And I've made those conversations as brief as was politely possible. He'd call and tell me all about how happy the two of you were and all about his family (none of whom I've ever met) and I'd say a nice little good-bye and that was that.

LAUREL   Then why'd you come up here?

ARNOLD   To see how my paint job was holding up. Y'know, I painted this room. Took me days. I was scared shitless of dripping on the floor; you know what a fussbudget Ed can be . . .

LAUREL   I'm sorry. I have no right to talk to you this way. I'm pushing you to admit something that you're obviously not ready to face.

ARNOLD   You're pushing me alright! But I don't think you realize toward what. Laurel . . . Are you happy with Ed?

LAUREL   The happiest I've ever been in my life.

ARNOLD   So what else do you want?

ALAN   To own a disco. [*Lights out on Arnold and Laurel, leaving
           Alan and Ed quite alone.*] I knew this guy, he was a few years
           older than me, who'd met this older guy who set him up in
           business. I figured that I could do the same. But when I made
           my entrance into the Big Apple, and believe me, a blue eyed
           blond of fourteen makes quite an entrance into any apple, I
           found that no one was interested in hearing about my busi-
           ness skills. In fact no one was interested in anything much
           besides my price tag for an evening. See, people with tastes
           for blue eyed blonds of fourteen are used to paying for it and
           consider a freebee suspicious if not downright immoral. And
           so, I became a hustler. I figured that I needed the affection
           more than they needed the money. Now, of course, things are
           different. But then . . . Anyway, I got along. The hustling
           led to some connections, the connections to my career, and
           the career to . . .

ED   Arnold!

ALAN   No, Arnold was more of a detour.

ED   That's Arnold.

ALAN   One night, I went out drinking with a friend and got more
           than usually polluted. Somehow I ended up in a lower east-
           side bar that had a drag show. Anyway, I wound up in a fight
           with this big black guy who threw me down on a table,
           jumped up on my chest and put a knife to my neck. Everyone
           was screaming and crowding around to watch me get cut,
           when all of a sudden there was silence and the crowd parted
           to make an aisle, and up through it like Moses through the
           Red Sea came this Amazon woman. You never seen anything
           like it. She was beautiful! Not like "pretty" beautiful, but like
           "mountain" beautiful. You know what I mean?

ED   That's Arnold!

ALAN   She put her hand out to the black guy like this, [*He demon-
           strates the gesture with haughty glare*] and he just handed over
           the knife and disappeared. No words, no nothing, just like
           that.

ED   When did you realize it was a guy?

ALAN   I was too drunk that night to realize that *I* was a guy. I sort of . . . fell onto that discovery the next morning.

ED '   [*Moving in closer*] How'd you feel about it?

ALAN   I'm with him, aren't I? [*Easing away. Holding up his glass.*] More please. [*Ed pours*] Now, you tell me about you. That's the whole reason we're here.

ED   Is it?

ALAN   Sure is. Arnold didn't want to come, but I wasn't going to let this chance to see my competition go by.

ED   I'm no competition. [*He moves closer again.*]

ALAN   Well, then my predecessor. Stop changing the subject. Tell me about you.

ED   Why don't you ask Arnold to tell you. I'm sure he's got lots to say on the subject.

ALAN   He has.

ED   And?

ALAN   He says you're a self-centered, insensitive, boring fool who wouldn't know love if it wore wings, a diaper and shot heart-shaped arrows at your butt.

ED   Meaning himself?

ALAN   Meaning himself. [*Lying down triumphantly*] Anything you'd care to add?

ED   No, that'll do. [*Lying down next to him*] And what do you think?

ALAN   I'll reserve my judgment until I can make a closer inspection.

ED   [*Putting his arm around Alan*] Close enough?

ALAN   [*Sitting up quickly*] Too close for comfort. You asked me to sit in the hay, not roll in it.

ED   [*Coming up behind him*] It was a two part question. I think you're very beautiful.

ALAN   I thought you were reformed.

ED   I'm not proposing marriage to you. [*Gently pulling him back*]
                If you want me to stop just say so. Do you? [*No response*] I
                didn't think so.
                [*The lights go out on them immediately leaving Arnold alone
                at the downstage right corner of the bed.*]

ARNOLD   I don't know when to stop. That's my problem. Me and my
                big fucking mouth. I didn't come up here to hurt her. I didn't
                even come up here to hurt him. (Though that would've been
                alright.) I was so proud of myself until now. I thought I was
                really handling this whole situation so maturely. I guess I was
                saving it all up for that. [*To Alan as if he were there*] I hope
                you're enjoying all this.

ALAN   [*From the dark*] Oh, I am.

ARNOLD   Good. 'Cause it's all your fault. Couldn't take no for an
                answer, you just had to come up here. Why couldn't I just
                keep my trap shut? I've always thought of myself as a kind
                person. Not saintly but generously thoughtful (in a bitchy
                sort of way). But since being here I have said nothing that
                hasn't hurt someone: you, Ed, Laurel, myself. Well, she asked
                for it. She begged for it . . . and boy did I give it to her. I
                was brilliant. Point after pointless point I proved beyond a
                shadow of a doubt that Ed has no idea that she even exists.
                That, to him, she's simply living proof of his normality.

ALAN   [*Joining Arnold, they fold clothing into a suitcase*] How many
                dishes did she break over your head?

ARNOLD   Not enough to keep me quiet.

ALAN   You elaborated?

ARNOLD   Ad infinitum. I quoted every report I could lay my brain on
                concerning bisexuality and its inherent unresolved immatur-
                ity, backing each prejudiced selection with a biased statis-
                tic . . .

ALAN   I love when you get technical.

ARNOLD   . . . . And finished her off with a quote from the man in
                question himself: That if all things were equal (she and I
                being the same sex), he never would have left me. Now, if
                that ain't dirty logic then what is?

ALAN   [*Feigning anguish*] Mercy! Mercy!

ARNOLD   Can that crap. This is for real.

ALAN   What're you getting so upset about? Who ever listens to you?

ARNOLD   There's always a first time. Come here and comfort me! Can't you see I'm disturbed?!?

ALAN   Why should I if you're such a rat?

ARNOLD   Because the innocent must suffer, not the guilty. This is America.

ALAN ·   [*Laughing*] You ain't so tough. [*Embracing*] That feel better?

ARNOLD   And she took it. Stood there staring me straight in the eye and listened to it all. Never argued, just nodded. God, you smell so good.

ALAN   Better than him?

ARNOLD   Now you're gonna start? [*Messing his hair*] He's jealous of you. Really. He told me so himself.

ALAN   Who isn't? I have you don't I? [*Embrace*] You shouldn't have disappeared with her all afternoon. How do you think I felt?

ARNOLD   How'd you feel?

ALAN   You just shouldn't've.

ARNOLD   What're you, a baby? I gotta sit and hold your hand?

ALAN   I came up here to be with you, not him. Let's get outta here.

The lights lower as a slide appears:

CODA

Alan slips under the covers, Laurel sits in the center, the phone rings.

ARNOLD   [*Answering in his sleep*] Hello?

ED   Hi. I woke you.

ARNOLD   Good guess. Hold on a second. [*He sits up and tries to shake the sleep.*] Hello? Listen I was gonna call you later to thank you for the weekend. [*Morning cough*] As you can hear, the country air's done wonders for me.

ED   I thought I'd call to make sure you two got home alright.

ARNOLD   Yeah, fine. We drove straight through.

ED   I really enjoyed having you here. So did Laurel.

ARNOLD   I'm glad. We did too.

ED   You know, we got a lot out of having you up here. We learned
           a lot about our relationship.

ARNOLD   You holding seminars?

ED   Couldn't you be nice?

ARNOLD   Sorry, morning breath and all.

ED   Is Alan there with you?

ARNOLD   No, he dropped me off then headed out to Queens to bring
           the car back to his mother. I guess he spent the night.

ED   Oh. But he'll be back tonight?

ARNOLD   I suppose. What's the difference?

ED   I was curious, that's all.

ARNOLD   Something wrong?

ED   Not at all.

ARNOLD   You sound funny.

ED   No. But I do have a favor to ask.

ARNOLD   Shoot.

ED   Well . . . Laurel went into the city this morning to spend a
           few days. Just to check on some classes . . . Anyway, I
           thought it'd be nice if you had her over to dinner or went out
           together for lunch or something. Just so she's not alone.

ARNOLD   Shit, look Ed, I'm really sorry I caused trouble . . .

ED   Oh, no. We didn't have words or anything. I just felt that it
           would be better if we both had time to think about our
           relationship.

ARNOLD   I understand.

ED   I know you do. I love her very much.

ARNOLD   Have you tried telling her that?

HARVEY FIERSTEIN *AND* DIANE TARLETON

HARVEY FIERSTEIN *AND* PAUL JOYNT

COURT MILLER, FISHER STEVENS *AND* HARVEY FIERSTEIN

ED   She's not like you, Arnold. She doesn't need to be reassured
            every hour on the hour.

ARNOLD   An admirable quality; to be sure.

ED   Will you talk to her?

ARNOLD   Don't worry about a thing.

ED   I appreciate it.

ARNOLD   Anything else?

ED   There is one thing more.

ARNOLD   Don't stop now.

ED   Did you have a chance to correct that list yet?

ARNOLD   What list?

ED   Of the things you want. Remember, I told you to erase the
            checkmark next to my name.

ARNOLD   [*Exasperated*] As a matter of fact, I haven't had the time. But
            don't you worry, I'll take care of it.

ED   Don't. I mean . . . I'd like it if you left the checkmark
            where it is.
            [*Laurel pops into the scene as Ed disappears under the covers.*]

LAUREL   So what'd you tell him?

ARNOLD   I told him I'd leave the checkmark but erase the name.

LAUREL   You didn't?!?

ARNOLD   No, I didn't. But I should've. I don't know, sometimes I get
            the feeling he's learning, but God, it's a struggle. You going
            back to him?

LAUREL   I don't think so. I don't know.

ARNOLD   What'd your shrink say?

LAUREL   Not much. Nothing, as a matter of fact, nothing. He just kept
            asking me what I want. Over and over again, "What do you
            want?", "What do you want?"

ARNOLD   And what did you tell him?

LAUREL   I told him I wanted him to shut up.

ARNOLD   [*Giggling*] You didn't.

LAUREL   [*Laughing too*] No, I didn't. But I should've. What do *you* want?

ARNOLD   I wanna beer.

LAUREL   You know what I mean.

ARNOLD   What do I want? What do I want? What do I want? Well, it would have to be something witty because you're depressed and it's not enough to be funny when talking to a depressed person. One must be cleverly diverting or at least playfully bawdy . . .

LAUREL   Your brain is hopelessly delinquent.

ARNOLD   That's what I want: A hopeless delinquent! No, I already got one of those.

LAUREL   Alan and you are wonderful together. I'm sure everything will work itself out.

ARNOLD   I didn't know there was anything that needed working out.

LAUREL   Didn't you two have words?

ARNOLD   None we haven't used before.

LAUREL   Oh. I thought that was why you returned last night instead of this morning.

ARNOLD   Not at all.

LAUREL   What happened between Alan and Ed doesn't bother you at all?

ED   [*Sitting up to one side*] You blurted it out just like that?

LAUREL   [*To Ed*] I thought he knew. I meant it as a friendly remark.

ARNOLD   [*To Alan*] With friends like her who needs newspapers?

ALAN   I tried to tell you . . .

ARNOLD   I must say, you picked a great time to start telling the truth.

LAUREL   [*To Arnold*] Why did you think I left?

ARNOLD   [*To Laurel*] I thought it was something I said.

LAUREL   Don't be silly.

ALAN   [*To Ed*] Are you going to tell Laurel?

ED   [*To Alan*] What I do is my own business.

LAUREL   [*To Arnold*] We respect each other's privacy.

ARNOLD   . . . and he still had energy for me. Oh, to be eighteen
            again! But, you and Alan didn't . . .

LAUREL   No! Why? He said we did?

ARNOLD   Well, I'm sure he meant it as a compliment. . . . to both of
            you.

ALAN   [*To Ed*] I thought an open relationship meant that you told
            each other everything.

ARNOLD   You saw them together?

LAUREL   No. Ed told me about it after you left. He came into the
            bedroom and said he had something to discuss . . . dis-
            cuss!? And he told me. He was crying. He said he was sorry—
            not that he'd done it, but that he had to tell me about it. I was
            dumbfounded. I didn't know which of us to comfort; who
            was hurting more. So, I sat there. We didn't say a word,
            occasionally catching each other's eye and looking away
            again. After a while he went down to the kitchen and I
            packed a bag and left. I hadn't planned on leaving . . . But,
            it seemed the right thing to do. There I was, packed, at the
            door . . . so I left.

ARNOLD   That wasn't very bright.

LAUREL   And what would you have done?

ARNOLD   I'd've shoved him head first into a meat grinder. But I
            would've hung around to see what came out the other end.

LAUREL   Arnold, you don't seem to be getting the drift of this at all.
            He made love to someone; your lover, with me not fifty feet
            away. What more reason would a person possibly need to
            walk out on someone?

ARNOLD   [*To Alan*] I have never felt so used in my life! I wanted to put
            a pillow over her face and snuff her out. [*Mocking*] "I hadn't
            planned on leaving." The gall! "What more reason would a
            person possibly need to walk out?" The nerve!!

LAUREL   So, this is the nursery. It's not at all what I'd expected from
           Ed's description. I like it though. It's got a coziness . . . a
           warmth. I can feel it.

ARNOLD   [*To Laurel*] Thanks.

LAUREL   If this is the nursery, does that make you the nurse?

ARNOLD   Registered with the A.M.A. You need one? [*Laurel nods and
           begins to cry*] Nurse Arnold to the rescue. [*He takes her in his
           arms like a baby.*] I accept Blue Cross, Blue Shield and Blue
           Nun. Hurts, huh?

LAUREL   Like a claw in my stomach. Just once in my life I'd like to
           have an affair go on the rocks after the passion wears off;
           when I'm bored with the routine, the sex, the talk. I'd love to
           know what it feels like to have the flame rekindled by jealousy
           instead of this . . . having the rug pulled out from under
           me like this. Just once I'd like to be standing on sure ground
           when the blow hits instead of crawling around on my hands
           and knees like a baby.

ARNOLD   You want a hell of a lot out of life. Don't'cha'? I'd settle for
           being able to say to someone, "I love you," and whether I
           meant it or not, finding them still in bed the next morning.

ALAN   All you had to do was ask me.

ARNOLD   Ask you what?

ALAN   Not to fool around with anyone else, and I wouldn't have.

LAUREL   But you never asked me.

ED   Because I wanted you to feel that you could.

ALAN   You mean, you wanted me to feel that *you* could. All those
           nights you spent out in them backrooms: How do you think I
           felt?

ARNOLD   That's not the same thing at all. I didn't even know those
           people's names.

ALAN   That makes a difference?

LAUREL   You mean you want me to see other men?

ARNOLD   No. But I want you to feel free to.

ALAN   I do. And I did. So, what are you so upset about?

ED   It's the kind of relationship you said you wanted.

LAUREL   Just because I said that's what I want doesn't mean that's
            what I want. I mean, that's what I want but that doesn't
            mean that I'm necessarily ready for it.

ALAN   You're being ridiculous.

ARNOLD   You telling me that you don't see any difference between my
            innocent jaunts to the backroom and your vile debauchery
            this weekend?

ALAN   Not really.

ARNOLD   Well. There you have it!

ALAN   There I have what?

ARNOLD   Don't be such a smart ass!

LAUREL   [*To Arnold*] It's my own fault for expecting something differ-
            ent. The only thing different about each of the affairs in my
            life is the way they dumped me. Not even the way so much as
            the words.

ARNOLD   I know what you mean. My favorite kiss-offs are those little
            speeches: "I really dig you, baby. You're the kind that I could
            really fall for. But, I'm not ready to fall so Adios."

LAUREL   I much prefer the continental version: "We've got a good
            thing going; let's not mess it up by getting too involved."

ARNOLD   How about, "Let's not make any promises we'll regret later?"

LAUREL   You ever hear the one about the trial separation?

ARNOLD   As often as I've heard about their reconciliation.

LAUREL   "I've got to try my wings."

ARNOLD   "I've got to repark the car."

LAUREL   "I've got to live free!"

ARNOLD   "She meant nothing to me!" Oops. Sorry.

LAUREL   That's alright. It's nothing I haven't heard before.

ARNOLD   Gee but it's GREAT to have someone else to blame. [*They both laugh.*]

LAUREL   I don't understand; how could Ed ever have let you get away?

ARNOLD   I'm lousy in bed. It's true. I don't relax enough. I guess I'm just an old fashioned kind of guy: I hardly ever enjoy sex with someone I know. So, you ready to call home?

LAUREL   I don't know. What do you think?

ARNOLD   I think I'm the wrong person to ask.

ALAN   [*Coupling with Arnold*] That's the first thing you've said all week that's made sense.

ARNOLD   Look who's talking.

LAUREL   [*Coupling with Ed*] I should at least give him a chance to explain.

ALAN   She'll stay with him. They were made for each other.

LAUREL   I owe him as much.

ARNOLD   It's wrong.

LAUREL   After all, what have I got to lose.

ARNOLD   It's all wrong.

LAUREL   Otherwise . . . What was it all for?

ARNOLD   I can't tell you how strongly I feel that it's wrong! [*They are alone in the light.*] You were wrong to do what you did! . . . though I know why you did. And Ed was wrong to do what he did! . . . though I know why he did. And Laurel was wrong to use what you two did!! . . . though I know why she did. And I was wrong to do everything I did! . . . but I did. I don't know, maybe it all evens out in the end. I mean, if two wrongs don't make a right . . . maybe four do.

ALAN   So the score's all evened up.

ARNOLD   I can't tell with these "Make 'em up as you go along" rules. Monogamy's a much easier system to keep track of.

ALAN   Well, look at it this way: Ed's got what he wants—a warm body in bed with a very attractive break in his routine. And Laurel's got what she wants—Ed in bed . . .

ARNOLD   With a million new fascinating problems to discuss with her shrink.

ALAN   And we've got what we want . . . each other.

ARNOLD   You're awful pushy for a kid who ain't old enough to pee straight.

ALAN   [*Lying back*] Come here and I'll show you how pushy.

ARNOLD   [*Delighted*] Just let me turn out the lights.

ALAN   Why do you wanna turn out the lights?

ARNOLD   Because, even in times like these one must retain a degree of the old cherished decorum.

ALAN   Well, aren't we civilized.

ARNOLD   Terribly!

ALAN   Wait. There's one more thing I'd like to ask you.

ARNOLD   [*Into his arms*] The answer is yes.

ALAN   But you don't know the question.

ARNOLD   Doesn't matter. I'm too tired to argue about anything so whatever it is the answer is yes.

ALAN   Good. Because I love you too.

ARNOLD   [*Pulling away*] Oh for God's sake, Alan, after everything we've been through this weekend . . .

ALAN   Oh, shut up! [*Embarrassed*] Can't you take a joke?

The music begins to play as Arnold sits up staring straight ahead in bewildered shock. As the bed begins to leave the stage he lies back into Alan's arms in hopeless surrender. Alan feeds him a piece of cake as the bed disappears offstage.

A slide:

EPILOGUE

The quartet music is joined by a piano. Upstage we see the small ornate stage and baby grand piano of a nightclub. The pianist is playing the introduction to a violent, angry love song. Arnold enters in rehearsal clothes carrying his music and sings the song. His is a passionate interpretation. The song ends.

ARNOLD   [*To pianist. Making a note on the score.*] That ought'a fog up
           their glasses and empty their mugs. We'll use it between "Cry
           Me A River" and "Who's Sorry Now." Just as a change of
           pace.

LAUREL   [*She's been watching from the wings*] God, you're depressing.

ARNOLD   Laurel? Oh, no!

LAUREL   Thanks a lot.

ARNOLD   No, I didn't mean: Oh no: not you. I meant: Oh no: you two
           had another fight.

LAUREL   Oh, no: not at all.

ARNOLD   Really?

LAUREL   You say that like you don't believe it.

ARNOLD   Oh, no.

LAUREL   Let's not start that again. Aren't you going to say hello?

ARNOLD   Hello. Sorry, but this just ain't my day. My maid called in
           sick, my cleaning came in late, we've got these new numbers
           to rehearse . . .

LAUREL   Maybe I'd better not bother you.

ARNOLD   No, stay. I could use a little gossip in the midst of all this
           reality. [*To pianist*] Five minutes, hon. [*Taking a chair off a
           little table*] Here, make yourself at home.

LAUREL   Oh, the man in front asked me to give you this. [*She hands
           him a small parcel.*]

ARNOLD   [*Taking down a chair for himself*] Thanks. Here sit down.

LAUREL   You really like that?

ARNOLD   [*Opening the package*] What?

LAUREL   Songs about suicide, lost love, growing old disgracefully.

ARNOLD   Pays the rent.

LAUREL   Funny, but I always imagined you'd sing comic songs.
           Y'know, novelty numbers.

ARNOLD   I'm strictly Torch. While all the other kids were listening to
           the Beatles, Sam the Sham and the Dave Clark Five, I was

home lip-synching Billie Holiday, Jane Froman and Helen Morgan. As I got older I switched to *Lucia di Lammemoor, Tosca* and *Manon.* But it was always tragic stuff. Something about taking all that misery and making it into something . . . Anyway, the audiences like it. I guess getting hurt is one thing we all have in common.

LAUREL   You sound like one of your songs.

ARNOLD   I am one of my songs. [*Taking out a leash and collar from the package*] Oh look, it's my wedding present to Alan.

LAUREL   And you told me you weren't into that stuff.

ARNOLD   It's for Alan's dog.

LAUREL   I didn't know he had a dog.

ARNOLD   He doesn't. But he will tomorrow when I give him one.

LAUREL   You got him a dog? What kind?

ARNOLD   Well, y'know they say that a dog grows to look like its master, or that a master grows to look like his dog . . . So, I got him a big, fat, home-loving St. Bernard. It should be quite a battle.

LAUREL   Perfect. So, you two are getting married?

ARNOLD   As married as two men can illegally get. Actually it's more of a contract signing party. After that weekend the four of us spent together we decided to draw up a few rules and regulations, just so we'd know where we stood with each other. Well, we've spent our every waking, non-working hour on this document and we're finally ready to sign it. [*Holds up a rolled up piece of parchment*]

LAUREL   That's wonderful. May I see it? [*She opens it*] It's one sentence long.

ARNOLD   Well, we had a little trouble agreeing on some issues. This is sort of a basic working philosophy which we can amend and elaborate on as we feel necessary.

LAUREL   [*Reading*] We, Arnold and Alan, being of sound mind and social-diseaseless bodies hereby swear to take equal responsibility for walking and feeding the dog.

ARNOLD   [*Taking it away*] Like I said, it's just a basis. Anyway, the
           ceremony's tomorrow after the show and we'd love for you to
           come.

LAUREL   I wish we'd known. But we've already made plans to take care
           of a few important things. Which brings me to my reason for
           coming to see you.

ARNOLD   . . . always a reason.

LAUREL   You know, now that it's time I don't know how to say it.

ARNOLD   Sounds serious.

LAUREL   It is.

ARNOLD   Be blunt.

LAUREL   Ed and I are engaged to be married.

ARNOLD   [*Blank*] Oh.

LAUREL   You and Alan, Ed and me. Kind of ironic, huh?

ARNOLD   That's the word for it. Well, congratulations. I'm sure you
           two will be very happy together.

LAUREL   Thank you.

ARNOLD   When was all this decided?

LAUREL   I guess about the same time you were drawing up your con-
           tract. We talked a lot when I went back to the farm; about
           what we wanted out of a relationship, what we wanted from
           each other . . . and we figured after that weekend . . .
           Well, if we could get through a thing like that and still be
           together then we could get through anything. Even marriage.

ARNOLD   I could hardly say I didn't expect it, but I could hardly say I
           did expect it . . . What I could say is that I'm happy for
           you. Hey, I'm gonna call Ed right now . . .

LAUREL   I'd rather you didn't. Ed doesn't know I'm here. As a matter
           of fact he's planning on coming by tonight to tell you himself.
           And I'd like to ask you not to mention my visit. After all, he
           did want to tell you first.

ARNOLD   Then why did you tell me?

LAUREL   I don't know. That's not true. I was scared that you'd say
           something negative—make fun of him or try to talk him out

of it. Arnold, everything's going so well between us, but Ed is still shaky. And the wrong word from you . . .

ARNOLD   That's ridiculous.

LAUREL   No, it's realistic.

ARNOLD   You're just being silly. Really you are. The two of you will get married and live happily ever after and I'm very happy for you. And just to prove it . . . I'll be a bridesmaid at the wedding. So, what color are we wearing?

LAUREL   Oh, it would mean so much to both of us to have you there, but the wedding is at my parents' home in Massachusetts and . . . it's really going to be small . . . so we're limiting the guests to just immediate family.

ARNOLD   That's alright; I look terrible in green.

LAUREL   I'm sorry, really. Well, I'd better let you get back to your rehearsal. I've kept you long enough. It was wonderful seeing you again. And as soon as we get set up we'll have you over for dinner or something.

ARNOLD   Sure. We'd love that.

LAUREL   You won't say anything to Ed?

ARNOLD   My wrists are sealed.

LAUREL   Pardon?

ARNOLD   An old fag joke.

LAUREL   Well, bye bye. Give my best to Alan. [*Laurel exits and Arnold returns to piano*]

ARNOLD   Hey Max, you know the wedding march? Never mind. Let's try the closing number.

[*The pianist begins to play as Arnold climbs up onto the piano.*]

It's over, concluded, expired, that's it.
I've had it, been through it, my limit's been hit.
It's not that I doubt your love for me,
Your passion or sincerity,
Your faith, hope, trust or charity,
What I doubt . . . is you.

You cheated, you lied, dear. You two-timed me twice.
And that makes four times, dear. And that isn't nice.
And now you've the nerve to say to me,
Your wife likes being one of three.
So I'll genteely answer thee:
Go blow it out your shoe.

I can't live on love alone.
Want somebody all my own.
I can't live on love alone.
You can argue but it's true,
Three can't live as cheap as two.
I can't live on love alone.

Fidelity is out of fashion,
Variety is everybody's passion.
Drugs can keep you copulating 'til you cash in.
And when you're through they'll bury you with your wife.

One night stands are not my quarry,
I signed up for repertory.
No I won't live on love alone.
Keep my number by the phone
Call me if you should atone.
But I can't live, no I can't live . . . on love alone.

[*The lights fade to black.*]

THE END

Widows
and
Children
First!

WIDOWS AND CHILDREN FIRST! premiered at La Mama E.T.C. on
October 25, 1979 with the following cast:

ARNOLD BECKOFF	*Harvey Fierstein*
DAVID	*Frederick Allen*
ED	*Will Jeffries*
MRS. BECKOFF	*Estelle Getty*

Directed by Eric Concklin
Stage Design by Bill Stabile
Lighting by Cheryl Thacker
Costumes by Carla Lawrence
Production Stage Manager: Richard Jakiel

CHARACTERS
Ed Reiss: Forty, handsome, with a disarming boyish charm and innocence.
David: Fifteen going on thirty. A wonderfully bright and handsome boy.
Arnold: Thirties, witty, personable and pleasant in appearance.
Mrs. Beckoff: Arnold's mother. Sixtyish. A real Jewish mother. A fighter.

TIME
Five years after the action of FUGUE IN A NURSERY.

SYNOPSIS OF SCENES
1) Arnold's apartment, 7 a.m. on a Thursday in June.
2) Same. 5 p.m. that day.
3) A bench in the park below, immediately following.
4) The apartment. 6 a.m. the next morning.

AUTHOR'S NOTE
PACE!!!!!!! and honesty.

Scene 1

*The stage is a realistically represented living/dining room and kitchenette.
There is an entrance door, a bathroom door and a hallway which leads to two
offstage bedrooms. It is the set of a conventional sit-com with a convertible
sofa, windows overlooking Central Park, and assorted objects and props.
There is also a mini-set for Scene 3 which is described herein. As the lights
come up, a radio is blaring Fanny Brice singing, "I'm Cooking Breakfast For
The One I Love." Ed is busily cooking. The song ends. . . .*

RADIO   It's seven-eighteen in the Big Apple and this is Hi Tide
        wishin' you a good, good Mornin'. [*A chorus of singers twitter,*
        "Good Morning, Good morning, Good Morning to you!"]
        And now for all you sleepy-heads what just can't shake them
        nighttime blues, number one on our hot-pick chart and guar-
        anteed to raise the dead . . . Edward O. Wilson's, "I Was
        Born This Way, What's Your Excuse." [*Music begins.*]

ED   [*Quickly changing to a mellower station*] There's a thought to
        start the day.

DAVID   [*From within the bathroom*] Arnold? You got anything I could
        put on my eye?

ED   [*Calling back*] He's in the bedroom.

DAVID   What?

ED   Arnold's still in the bedroom.

DAVID   Never mind, I found somethin'.

ED   [*Hollering down the hall*] Arnold, you up? Breakfast is on the
        table.

DAVID   What?

ED   I was talking to Arnold. [*An explosion in the kitchen*]

ARNOLD [*Offstage*] What the hell was that?

ED   [*Running to kitchen*] I think the coffee's ready.

ARNOLD [*Enters in bathrobe and bunny-shaped slippers*] And a "Good
        Morning, Good Morning, Good Morning to you." You're
        making breakfast? Aren't you an angel. Smells terrible.

ED   My specialty: Eggs, onions and Kippered Herring en casserole.

ARNOLD   Toast for me, I'm on a diet.

ED   Since when?

ARNOLD   Since I heard the specialty. [*Yelling down hall*] David, you up yet?

ED   He's in the throne room.

ARNOLD   [*Knocks on door*] Hurry up, Sugar-Puss, you'll be late for school.

ED   You look well rested.

ARNOLD   I feel like freeze-dried death. [*Sees mess*] Ed, since when do you make coffee in a pressure cooker?

ED   The water boils faster.

DAVID   [*Through crack in door*] Everybody ready? Stand back from the door and hang onto your apron strings 'cause here I come. [*Enters modeling a three piece suit*] Well? What'cha think?

ARNOLD   [*As Ed whistles approval*] What's the occasion? Ms. Schnable isn't due till next week.

DAVID   But your mother is due today. Think she'll like me?

ARNOLD   Who'd dare not like my baby?

DAVID   And look, I put some gook on. You can't even see the black eye.

ARNOLD   [*Examining*] When I think of that kid hitting you, I wanna tear down to that school and beat the shit outta him.

ED   [*Serving the food*] Your maternal instincts are incredible.

DAVID   I can take care of myself.

ARNOLD   I see.

DAVID   Would you stop.

ED   What'd the two of you fight about anyway?

DAVID   He called me something I didn't like, so I slugged him. [*Helping Arnold fold the couch*]

ED   So how'd you end up with the black-eye?

DAVID   I didn't slug him fast enough.

ARNOLD   That's my son, The Champ.

DAVID   [*Posing*] That's me, Champ David.

ED   What was it he called you?

DAVID   A douche bag.

ARNOLD   How fifties.

ED   Soup's on!

ARNOLD   [*Exiting to bathroom*] You stay away from that kid today. I
          ain't got no money to buy no new suit.

DAVID   He's somethin' ain't he? What's with this dentist music?
          [*Switches to rock station. It is the same song only discoed.*]
          Much better.

ED   [*Holding out chair*] May I seat you, sir?

DAVID   Don't mind if you do. [*Sits*] What died in here?

ED   Breakfast. [*Holding plate over David's head*] I cooked it my-
          self. Any complaints?

DAVID   From me? Are you kidding? You know me, always ready for a
          gastronomic adventure. [*Ed sets down plate*] Looks wonder-
          ful. Could you pass the salt? How'd you sleep?

ED   The couch and I aren't speaking.

DAVID   It's only your fourth night. You'll get used to it. Could you
          pass the pepper? I slept on it for weeks while we worked on
          my room, and I'm still walking.

ED   I'll probably be able to find a place by the weekend.

DAVID   What's your rush? Can I have the ketchup? It's great having
          you here. Could you pass the mustard?

ED   Something wrong with the food?

DAVID   Not at all. Very tasty. Can I have the mayo, please? [*Ed
          shoots a look*] Hold the mayo. [*Tastes it*] Mmmmmm. Deli-
          cious. Oh, I forgot, your wife called.

ED   When?

DAVID   Middle of the night. I tried to wake you but you were out of it. I told her you'd call back in the morning.

ED   What time did she call?

DAVID   Must'a been around two. Somethin' about some papers for you to sign.

ED   Thanks. I'd better call. Help yourself to seconds, there's plenty.

DAVID   And I was worried. [*Ed goes to phone*] You sure are a heavy sleeper. The phone rang five times.

ED   What were you doing up so late?

DAVID   Answering the phone.

ED   [*Into phone*] Hello, Laurel? What's up . . . Couldn't that have waited til morning? . . . I don't think it's fair to wake the whole house. . . .

ARNOLD   [*Entering*] Hey, Champ, remember to bring back your report card. I signed it.

DAVID   Where'd you put it?

ARNOLD   By the door.

DAVID   Is Ms. Schnable really coming next week?

ARNOLD   Every third Thursday for the next three months. So stay outta trouble and pray that eye heals. I wish this damned probation period was over already. Gives me the creeps havin' someone check up on us all the time.

DAVID   What's the rush? When the adoption papers come through we stop gettin' the Foster care checks and we need the money.

ARNOLD   You may find this hard to believe, but I didn't take you in for the money.

DAVID   Then you're the first.

ARNOLD   [*Seeing Ed*] Who's on the phone?

DAVID   Ed.

ARNOLD   I thought I recognized the voice.

ED   . . . Laurel, I wish you wouldn't. . . . Not on the phone!

ARNOLD   There's nothing more frustrating that a one-sided conversation.

DAVID   There's another kind?

ED   . . . I really don't want to discuss this now. . . . Because, there are other people in the room.

DAVID   Don't mind us. [*Arnold swats him.*]

ED   . . . Can we please talk about this later? . . . Hello? . . . Laurel, are you there? . . . For God's sake, are you crying?

ARNOLD   [*Under his breath*] Animal.

ED   Laurel, please. I'll come over and we can talk. . . . I don't know when. This afternoon. I don't know . . . Alright, I'll see you then. . . . Bye Bye. [*Hangs up*]

DAVID   She gave you a hard time, huh? [*Arnold swats him again.*] Ow! That hurt.

ARNOLD   [*Big smile*] Want some coffee?

ED   No, I'm fine. After four days of those calls I think I'm getting used to them. I mean, I understand why she calls; she's confused, alone . . . What I can't understand is her damned crying.

ARNOLD   Of course it's just a wild guess, but do you suppose it's because she's confused and alone?

ED   Well, I don't see why. This separation wasn't all my idea.

ARNOLD   Look, Ed, I realize this is a trying time for you and I'll gladly supply a place to sleep, a home-thrown meal and all the amoral support I can muster, but you've got to keep the gory details to yourself.

ED   [*Grandly*] Ah, what price compassion!?!

ARNOLD   Fifty bucks an hour and I don't take credit cards.

ED   Fifty?

ARNOLD   Hey, talk's cheap, but listening'll cost ya'. Buck up, Bronco, things are bound to get easier.

ED   Oh, I know. I just wish she wouldn't carry on like that. You wouldn't believe the crazy accusations she was making . . .

ARNOLD   Ed, I'm serious. I really don't want to hear about it.

ED   [*Mock pout*] Some friend you are.

ARNOLD   I'm your ex-lover, Ed, not your friend.

DAVID   Oooooh. The heavy stuff. And it ain't even eight o'clock.

ARNOLD   [*Turning David's head back to his plate*] Don't talk with your mouth full.

DAVID   But my mouth's . . . [*Arnold glares.*] Is full. Very full.

ARNOLD   I didn't say that to be mean. Really. But I can't help remembering a phone call not unlike that one from someone in this very room, if you get my drift.

ED   Didn't think of that.

ARNOLD   Well, do. Please do. And please don't ask for any advice, 'cause you don't want to hear what I have to say.

DAVID   Heartbreaker. [*Arnold glares.*] I'm eating. I'm eating.

ARNOLD   All this and my Mother too.

ED   Well, I'll see Laurel this afternoon and hopefully end these midnight calls.

ARNOLD   That would be lovely. And while you're there could you see if she'd mind letting you stay with her Wednesday night? The Department of Child Welfare will be arriving early in the person of Our Ms. Schnable and I've got enough to explain without you on the couch.

ED   I'm good enough for your mother but not for David's social worker?

ARNOLD   It has nothing to do with being good enough. Ms. Schnable frowns on casual cohabitation.

ED   Casual? We've known each other for six years.

ARNOLD	Four of which you spent married to another woman. [*To David*] Take a glass of milk.
ED	[*Pouring David's milk*] I get it, it's not me she'll object to but my bisexuality.
ARNOLD	Could we please leave your perverted preferences unpurported this joyous morn?
ED	Bigot!
ARNOLD	Reactionary Chicken shit!
DAVID	Please, not in front of the child.
ED	I could lie and tell her I'm gay.
ARNOLD	Come on.
ED	Don't you think I could make a convincing homosexual?
DAVID	You could make this convincing homosexual.
ARNOLD	David! Besides, if she thought you were gay, she'd never believe you slept on the couch.
ED	I could show you the scars.
ARNOLD	I could show you the door.
DAVID	I could show you a good time.

ED and ARNOLD: David!!

DAVID	Well, I'd love to sit and chat with you grown-up types, but we straight C students pride ourselves on our punk-tuality.
ARNOLD	Go brush your teeth.
DAVID	Oh, Maaaaaaaa!
ARNOLD	Don't you, 'Oh, Ma," me. March. And don't call me Ma in front of my mother. [*David exits. Ed giggles.*] Having a good time?
ED	Sorry, but you do act like his mother.
ARNOLD	Guess I do. But this parent act's still new to me. I can't quite get the hang of being mother, father, friend and confessor all rolled into one.
ED	You're doin' great.

ARNOLD   Think so?

ED   You're the best Mother-father-friend-confessor I've ever
          seen. You've just got to let go a little more.

ARNOLD   I will. Geez, I can't wait for my mother to get here; I can
          Mother-smother David, she can Mother-smother me . . .

ED   And I can Mother-smother referee.

ARNOLD   Laugh now Leroy, but we're gonna need one. Y'know, this
          stuff smells awful, but it tastes much worse.

ED   Be nice or I'll tell people it's your recipe.

ARNOLD   You don't have to threaten me twice.

ED   I'm enjoying being here with you and David enormously. I
          want you to know that.

ARNOLD   Good.

ED   You ever wonder what things would be like if I'd never met
          Laurel?

ARNOLD   That all depends, did I meet Alan?

ED   Of course not. If I didn't meet Laurel you wouldn't have met
          Alan.

ARNOLD   Oh. So that's how it works. Well, did I adopt David?

ED   That's what I'm asking. Would we have stayed together and
          would we have adopted David?

ARNOLD   How should I know?

ED   Well, didn't you ever wonder?

ARNOLD   Ed, I have enough trouble with the "What now's" without
          starting in on the "What if's."

ED   Yeah, but haven't you ever thought about what things would
          be like if we'd stayed together?

ARNOLD   I guess so. When Alan died I thought about a lot of crazy
          things. I'm sure you were among them.

ED   And?

ARNOLD   I don't know. Why, what do you think?

ED   I think we might've been very happy together. It's possible.

ARNOLD   It's also possible that it could be me you just walked out on.

ED   I didn't just walk out. And who just said they didn't want to discuss this?

ARNOLD   Who's discussing? I'm simply pointing out a certain pattern a certain person seems to have fallen into.

ED   People do make mistakes.

ARNOLD   I wanna write that down.

ED   . . . And sometimes they are even forgiven for them.

ARNOLD   Oh, don't be so melodramatic. I forgave you years ago. I don't think I could've been happy with Alan if I hadn't.

ED   Maybe you and your Mother should spend some time alone. I can still find a hotel.

ARNOLD   You're staying here and that's an order. You wouldn't leave me unprotected at a time like this would you? Of course you would. But you ain't gonna. My mother isn't going to feature the idea of my becoming a father, and your professional opinion as an American educator will prove invaluable.

ED   She'll say I'm prejudiced.

ARNOLD   She'll say a lot of things. You'll learn not to listen. More coffee?

ED   [*Hands his cup*] Please.

ARNOLD   [*Making coffee and cleaning up*] My mother's alright. Basically. When I was a kid we had a healthy Mother/Son relationship. A delicate blend of love, concern and guilt. We never talked much but when we did we kept things on an honest level. I mean, I told her I was gay when I was thirteen.

ED   You knew when you were thirteen?

ARNOLD   When I was thirteen I knew everything. Senility set in sometime after. And look at me now: On the threshold of thirty I need a calculator to write a check, a cookbook to fry an egg and Dial a Prayer to do the rest. [*To David*] Hurry up in there you'll be late.

DAVID   [*Offstage*] Don't rush an artist.

ARNOLD   What was I saying?

ED   Something about your mother.

ARNOLD   My mother: The Rita Hayworth of Brighton Beach. We always kept an open line of communication, that is until my father died; then, I don't know, something happened, she clammed up. I mean, we saw each other more than ever, and we spoke daily on the phone, but somehow we managed to say less than ever. It became a contest to see who could talk most but say least.

ED   It's called Adult Conversation.

ARNOLD   Thank you Tom Snyder. Where was I?

ED   Your mother.

ARNOLD   My mother: The Sylvia Sydney of Bay Twenty-fifth street. I think the root of it was my father's death. She refused to talk about it, or about how she was coping alone. But Alan and I were living together then, so I always had a source of subject matter in him.

ED   She knew Alan?

ARNOLD   Oh, yeah. And they got along as long as I didn't call him my lover. She preferred to call him my "Friend." Anyway, she retired, moved to Florida which reduced our relationship to weekly phone calls and biannual visitations. And then Alan died and I was expected to observe the same vow of silence about him as she had about my father. So we've learned to make meaningful conversation from the weather, general health and my brother's marital status. I never even told her how Alan was killed. She assumed it was a car accident and I didn't bother correcting her.

ED   So now you don't know how to tell her about David.

ARNOLD   Oh she knows about David. But she assumed he was my roommate and I . . .

ED   . . . You didn't bother correcting her.

ARNOLD   It's not the telling that frightens me. But I shake when I think of the long muzzled floodgates of Motherly advice that will unleash when she gets wind of this.

ED   How bad could it possibly be?

ARNOLD   Stick around kid.

DAVID   [*Entering*] How's these? [*Big smile*] And look, I'm taking the brush with me so's I can give them a swipe before my big entrance. Think Granny'll be impressed?

ARNOLD   David, you can put your elbows on the table, use vile and abusive language, even pass gas loudly during conversation. But whatever you do . . . Don't call her Granny!

DAVID   You could save yourself a load of grief if you'd just let me break the good news to her.

ARNOLD   Thanks, but I've heard your subtle mouth at work.

DAVID   Don't say I didn't offer. [*Phone rings*] I'll get it.

ED   [*To Arnold*] You want tea?

ARNOLD   Why not?

DAVID   [*Into phone*] Sister Arnold's House of Hope. You pay, we pray. Brother David speaking.

ARNOLD   [*Grabs phone*] Give me that. Hello? . . . Oh, hi Murray . . . No, that was David's idea of discretion.

DAVID   Think I have a future in the Diplomatic Corps?

ARNOLD   Hang on a sec. [*To David*] Don't you ever answer the phone like that again. What if this was Ms. Schnable? Have you got a comb? [*He produces one.*] A handkerchief? [*He moans.*] March!

ED   [*Handing tea to Arnold as David reads report card*] A handkerchief? Really Arnold.

DAVID   What the hell is this? [*Reads from card*] "I'm proud of his improvement and am sure he'll do even better on his finals."

ARNOLD   It said "Parent's Comments" and I had to write something.

DAVID   No you didn't. [*Storms to bedroom*]

ARNOLD   Murray, can I call you back after I get my little men off to work? OK, I'll call . . . David! Hang up that extension!

. . . No, you can't have a divorce. We're not married. . . . Murray? I'll call you back. [*Hangs up*] Alright, what'd I do wrong now?

ED   The kids like to brag that they forged their parent's signatures. But if there's a sensible comment like that then everyone will know it's the real thing.

ARNOLD   How was I supposed to know? God, he makes me feel old.

ED   Don't worry about it. What time is the Great Arrival?

ARNOLD   I don't know. I figure around noon.

DAVID   [*Enters with hanky*] I'm gettin' outta here before you think of something else.

ARNOLD   Where are your school books?

DAVID   In school.

ARNOLD   How'd you do your homework?

DAVID   Astral projection.

ARNOLD   You forgetting something?

DAVID   What now?

ARNOLD   Don't I get a kiss goodbye?

DAVID   [*Laughs*] You're unreal. [*Warm hug and kiss*] I love you.

ARNOLD   Me too. Now get outta here. You're late.

DAVID   [*Exiting*] Have a nice day, Ed. You too . . . Ma. [*Out*]

ED   Men kissing. What's this world coming to?

ARNOLD   My father and brother and I all kissed. It's called affection. Aren't you going to work?

ED   It's Brooklyn Day. My school's closed.

ARNOLD   Only the Brooklyn schools?

ED   And Queens.

ARNOLD   Queens too? Sounds like Affirmative Action at work. [*Sees Ed clearing dishes*] That's alright. I'll do them.

ED   Then I'll go for the papers. Maybe I'll get a lead on an
            apartment.

ARNOLD   Hurry back. I ain't facin' her alone. Do you and your mother
            get along?

ED   Sure. No problem. That is as long as I remember to call her
            every now and then. And send her a card on her Birthday.
            And Mother's Day. And Christmas. Oh, and of course
            there's Valentine's Day, and St. Patrick's Day, Labor Day,
            Thanksgiving, Easter, Fourth of July, Election Day and
            Christopher Columbus' Birthday.

ARNOLD   You forgot Halloween.

ED   That's her Anniversary.

ARNOLD   How romantic.

ED   Where's my blue jacket?

ARNOLD   My room, left side. [*Ed exits.*] Ed? You ever tell your folks you
            were gay?

ED   [*Reentering*] But I'm not.

ARNOLD   Alright, bisexual. Don't be so technical. I ain't Kinsey.

ED   No.

ARNOLD   Never?

ED   You need anything from the store?

ARNOLD   Wait a minute. I mean, I know you were in the closet when
            we were together, but I figured once you got married you'd
            feel secure enough to tell them.

ED   Once I got married there was nothing to tell them. [*Defen-
            sive*] And I wasn't in the closet.

ARNOLD   Ed, when the only people who know you're gay are the ones
            you're gaying with, that's called in the closet.

ED   Arnold, you may enjoy broadcasting your sexual preferences
            but I happen to believe that who I sleep with is my business
            and not the world's.

ARNOLD   We'll discuss the world later. I'm asking about your mother.

ED   Why put them through that?

ARNOLD   Through what?

ED   Making them feel that in some way they failed me or did something wrong. You know the trip.

ARNOLD   But you could explain to them that they had nothing to do with it. Well, not that way, anyway.

ED   They'd still be miserable. Besides, I really don't think it's any of their business.

ARNOLD   You told them about Laurel didn't you?

ED   We were married.

ARNOLD   You lived together for a year first. You sayin' they didn't know about her 'til after the wedding?

ED   Arnold, you told your parents, they accepted it and I'm very happy for all of you. Alright? Jesus. Your mother flies in for a visit and I get a Gay Consciousness Raising lecture.

ARNOLD   You have a Prim-Evil attitude about your sexuality, Mr. Reiss.

ED   Enough?

ARNOLD   And they wonder why we broke up.

ED   Arnold, you have nothing to worry about. Believe me, your mother will see you and David together and will be pleased with both of you.

ARNOLD   You really think I'm doing good with him?

ED   You've taken a punk kid who's spent the last three years on the streets and in juvenile court and turned him into a home-living, fun-loving, school-going teenager in all of six months. Yes, I think you're doing good with him.

ARNOLD   I wish Alan was here. He would'a been great with the kid.

ED   I'll see you later.

ARNOLD   Don't be too long.

ED   [*Exiting*] Give me an hour.

ARNOLD   See ya. [*Runs to door*] Ed? We need milk! Skimmed!!

              [*The phone rings. Arnold grunts and answers.*]

ARNOLD   Hello? . . . Oh, hi, Murray. . . . Not much. The usual assortment of early morning crises. What's up by you?

ED   [*Tears back into the room*] Arnold, she's here!

ARNOLD   Hang on, Murr. [*To Ed*] What?

ED   She's here. She's headed up the stairs.

ARNOLD   Can't be. It's too early.

ED   There's a woman on the stairs checking all the apartment numbers.

ARNOLD   What'd she look like?

ED   [*Indicating*] This tall, this wide, carrying a suitcase and a shopping bag.

ARNOLD   May Day, Murray! I'll call you back.

ED   Calm down Arnold. [*As Arnold runs around the room*]

ARNOLD   She can't see the place looking like this. She'll walk through the door and head straight for the vacuum cleaner.

MA   [*In the open doorway*] Well, I might change my shoes first.

ARNOLD   Ma. Hi. Come on in.

MA   [*Friendly to Ed*] Hello. You must be David.

ED   No, I'm Ed.

MA   [*Taking back her extended hand*] How do you do. I'm the mother.

ARNOLD   [*Taking her bags*] I really didn't expect you this early.

MA   Obviously.

ED   [*Backing out*] Well, I've got to be off. Lovely meeting you, Mrs. Beckoff. I'll remember the milk. [*Out. Then back in.*] Skimmed. [*Out*]

MA   Nice looking boy. Who is he?

ARNOLD   That's Ed . . .

MA   That's enough. (For now.) I'm sorry I snapped at him but that bus-ride from the airport. . . . I had to stand the whole way. There wasn't a man on that bus would give me his seat.

I'm telling you, Arnold, Women's Liberation is giving me varicose veins. So, let me look at you. How do you feel? You look good.

ARNOLD   Good compared to the last time you saw me.

MA   The last time I saw you was at your friend's funeral. You're supposed to look lousy at funerals; it shows respect. You could stand a shave.

ARNOLD   I just got up. Coffee?

MA   A glass of tea. And a can of Lysol. What's that stench?

ARNOLD   Ed cooked breakfast.

MA   So I know he's not the cook. Pretty wallpaper.

ARNOLD   It's not wallpaper. I stenciled the design.

MA   Next time use wallpaper. Covers a multitude of sins. Looks nice enough, but why you'd give up that lovely place in Brooklyn to move to Manhattan, God only knows.

ARNOLD   The other place had one bedroom. We needed two.

MA   I thought your roommate's name was David.

ARNOLD   It is. He isn't here right now.

MA   Three men, two bedrooms . . . I'll have my tea first.

ARNOLD   Ed's transitory. The sofa's a convertible. Honey?

MA   Lemon. I brought my own Sweet and Low . . . from the plane. You don't get much light here.

ARNOLD   We get what you call "indirect semi-shade." It's good for the plants.

MA   So's manure. Looks comfortable. How do you find the roaches?

ARNOLD   I turn on the lights. [*A little laugh at his little joke*]

MA   Arnold, when a man's with his friends he makes wife jokes. When he's with his wife he makes mother jokes. And when he's with his mother . . . he lets her make the jokes. [*Arnold gets the message.*] You speak to your brother?

ARNOLD   He was over for dinner last week.

MA   He brought a girl?

ARNOLD   Andrea.

MA   He's still seeing her? Any talk of marriage?

ARNOLD   You'll see him tomorrow, you can ask yourself.

MA   And be accused of meddling? Bite your tongue.

ARNOLD   [*Entering with tea tray, Ma is seated on sofa*] Are you getting shorter?

MA   No, I'm sitting down. So, who's this Ed?

ARNOLD   A friend. Tell me about Florida. Anyone special in your life?

MA   Not particularly. You mean Ed's a friend-friend or a euphemism friend?

ARNOLD   He used to be a euphemism, now he's just a friend. Why aren't you seeing anyone?

MA   Because the only ones who ask me out are old men and the one thing I don't need is to become a nursemaid for some *alta-kakah.*

ARNOLD   Don't you meet any men your own age?

MA   In Miami Beach? If he's not your friend why's he cooking your breakfast?

ARNOLD   You never cook for your friends?

MA   Not breakfast. Didn't you used to have a friend named Ed who got married?

ARNOLD   You've got a great tan.

MA   He's a teacher?

ARNOLD   And a great memory.

MA   The girl was too, right? They've got a house in the country.

ARNOLD   Incredible.

MA   I remember thinking, "Now there's a man with his head on straight." What's he doing cooking your breakfast?

ARNOLD   He and his wife have separated. He's staying here 'til he can find a place of his own.

MA   Separated? How come?

ARNOLD   I don't know.

MA   Come on, the man's living with you. He must've said some-
            thing.

ARNOLD   I didn't ask and he didn't volunteer.

MA   You're involved?

ARNOLD   No!

MA   Arnold?

ARNOLD   Ma?

MA   So why's he staying here?

ARNOLD   Because he asked if he could and I said yes.

MA   You must admit, it sounds a little queer: A man leaves his wife
            to move in with his old . . . friend.

ARNOLD   He's spending a few nights on my couch. What's the big
            deal?

MA   No big deal. But, you'd think he'd stay by friends that have
            more in common.

ARNOLD   What does that mean?

MA   You know; someone he met after the marriage.

ARNOLD   Maybe he needed to get away from all of that.

MA   You mean he's still . . . [*Makes a motion with her hand*]?

ARNOLD   Can we talk about the weather now?

MA   I'm glad you reminded me. [*Heads for her shopping bag*] Your
            mother! If I didn't have my head screwed on . . . I baked
            you some cookies. [*Produces a tin*] Fresh from the Sunshiney
            State. Take a whiff; you can smell Miami.

ARNOLD   David'll love these.

MA   I didn't know what to bring. I hadn't seen the place to know
            what you need.

ARNOLD   [*Friendly and confident now*] Oh, I didn't show you . . .

[*Takes out an afghan*] Look what I'm making. I took a class in weaving and crocheting at night school. Isn't it beautiful?

MA   I'm telling you . . . !

ARNOLD   I made it for out here. Y'know, for taking a nap on the couch. I wanna make one for my bedroom too. You like it?

MA   [*Trying to look away*] Nice.

ARNOLD   Pretty design, huh?

MA   It's fairy nice.

ARNOLD   [*The wind knocked out of him*] Well, maybe you should go unpack. You can put your things in my room.

MA   How are we arranging all of this?

ARNOLD   You'll sleep in my room, David in his room and Ed and I can share the couch.

MA   Wouldn't it be easier if I slept on the couch? That way you'll have your privacy.

ARNOLD   We don't need privacy.

MA   How about if you shared David's room?

ARNOLD   Did you see my cigarettes around?

MA   You still smoke? Shame on you. [*Arnold heaves a heavy sigh*] What's the matter, *sheyna boyalah?* You didn't sleep good?

ARNOLD   I'm fine. Just give me a minute to get myself together.

MA   Go on, get yourself together. I could use a get together myself. [*Deep breath*] Arnold, where's the dog? He didn't come to say hello.

ARNOLD   I had to give him away. He used to sit by the door and whine all day and night, waiting for Alan to come home. I couldn't take it so I gave him to Murray. [*Referring to stack of papers she has unpacked*] What's all that?

MA   Don't ask me why, they forwarded some of your mail to me.

ARNOLD   Anything I should know about?

MA   Garbage. But there's a letter from Ernie the insurance man. You canceled your policy?

ARNOLD   One of them.

MA   You need money? You know I'm always good for a loan.

ARNOLD   Thanks but things are fine.

MA   Meanwhile you lost out on a very good deal. You wouldn't see a policy like that again.

ARNOLD   What do I need with a twenty-five thousand dollar life insurance policy?

MA   Now you don't need it, but someday . . . ? You never know; you might meet a nice girl . . .

ARNOLD   Maaaa!

MA   You never know. Look at your friend Ed.

ARNOLD   I'm looking. He's separated.

MA   Separated, but not divorced. Believe me, you never know.

ARNOLD   Believe me. I know.

MA   What's the matter; you don't want children?

ARNOLD   Not the kind you mean.

MA   The kind I mean have two arms, two legs, a mother, father and Chicken Pox. How many kinds are there?

ARNOLD   You'd be surprised.

MA   Arnold, you and your brother are the last of the Beckoffs.

ARNOLD   So?

MA   Don't you feel you have a duty to continue the family name?

ARNOLD   Not particularly. Anyway, there's always my brother. I'm sure there'll be lots of little Beckoffs running around.

MA   And what if he only has girls?

ARNOLD   [*Thinks a moment*] I know a good surgeon.

MA   I don't get you?

ARNOLD   Why don't you unpack while I take a shower and shave. And when I'm dressed we can sit and have a lonng talk.

MA   A "Lonnng" talk? I feel a gray hair growing in.

ARNOLD   It's not that bad. Let me help with your bags.

MA   I can manage.

ARNOLD   It's the room on the right. Shit, I didn't have time to make the bed.

MA   Take your shower. I'll do it.

ARNOLD   There's fresh linen in the closet at the end of the hall.

MA   [*Waving him on*] Go. I'll get by.

ARNOLD   I won't be long. [*Exits*]

MA   [*Gathering her things*] You see, Jack? They still need the old Mama. [*Exiting*] Just think, if I wasn't here . . . who would make the beds?
         [*David enters through the front door, slowly, peeking in first. Seeing a deserted room, he enters fully and looks around. He spots the shopping bag.*]

DAVID   She has arrived. But where are she? [*Looks in kitchen, under table, goes to bathroom door and listens*] We got us a live one. [*Arnold hums a bit of something.*] Wrong one. [*He is having fun. He tiptoes to the hall and exits . . . A moment of silence, then a shriek. David runs out of the hall pursued by Ma who is swinging at him with her purse.*] Mrs. Beckoff, please. I'm not a burglar!

MA   Then what are you; some kind of weirdo who gets a kick watching middle-aged women strip beds?

DAVID   I'm not a weirdo. Believe me.

MA   Then you're a rapist. [*She screams again.*]

DAVID   What would a rapist be doing in a three-piece suit?

MA   How should I know? Maybe you got a wedding after.

ARNOLD   [*Entering, dripping in a robe*] What the . . . David! What are you doing out of school?

MA   This is your roommate?

DAVID   Charmed I'm sure.

MA   You know that "lonnng" talk we're gonna have? It just got lonnnnnnnger.

ARNOLD   What are you doing home?

DAVID   I forgot, I had a double period of gym and no uniform. So I tole' Mr. Kelley about your mother comin' and he said I could come home 'til after lunch.

ARNOLD   Just like that?

DAVID   Well, . . . you gotta call and say it's O.K. Wasn't that nice of him?

ARNOLD   [*Sees his mother's puzzled face*] We'll discuss this later. [*Trying to smile*] Ma, this is David.

MA   So I gathered.

ARNOLD   [*Long uncomfortable pause*] O.K. So, now we all know each other.

MA   Arnold, you're dripping on my shoe.

ARNOLD   Oh. How about this: You go finish unpacking, I'll go finish my shower, and you go start lunch . . . ?

DAVID   It's only nine o'clock.

ARNOLD   [*Parental order*] When I tell you to do something . . . [*Catches mother staring*] Well, I'm going to dry off now.

MA   You do that.

ARNOLD   [*Slowly backing out*] So, you'll unpack right? you'll make lunch, right? and I'll . . .

MA   Dry up.

ARNOLD   Right. [*Takes a last look, crosses himself and exits.*]

DAVID   [*Pause*] Would you like a drink?

MA   Maybe later. I'm sorry I hit you.

DAVID   No sweat. I usually charge, but seein' how you're family . . . [*He laughs.*]

MA   You have quite a little sense of humor. Shall we sit down?

DAVID   Sure. [*They do.*]

MA   Tell me, David, you go to school?

DAVID   Yeah. [*Sees cookies*] You make these?

MA	Help yourself. [*He does, by the handful*] So, you go to college.
DAVID	High school.
MA	[*Her heart!*] High School. How nice. [*Hopeful*] Senior year?
DAVID	Freshman.
MA	That's very sweet. Tell me, David, just how old are you?
DAVID	Sixteen. . . . in two months. [*Sees her dying*] Something wrong?
MA	Not at all. Sixteen . . . in two months . . . that's wonderful. You have your whole life ahead of you . . . while mine's flashing before my eyes.
DAVID	[*Chomping away*] Good stuff.
MA	[*At first she thinks he referred to her life, then . . .*] Thank you. David, it's none of my business, of course, but don't you think you're a little young to be out in the world all alone?
DAVID	No. But, the judge did, so here I am.
ARNOLD	[*Sticking his head out*] Everything alright out here?
MA	[*Choking*] Fine, dear. Keep drying. [*Arnold withdraws.*]
DAVID	You like the place? We cleaned all week for you. Sorry I didn't get back to see your face when you got here.
MA	That face couldn't compare to this one.
DAVID	I would'a taken the whole morning off, but you know Arnold . . . Hey, he better hurry up and call the school. Mr. Kelley'll think I was jivin' him.
MA	Does Arnold make all your excuses at school?
DAVID	[*Enjoying the game*] Sure. Who else?
MA	Who else, indeed. I've got an idea: Why don't I call the school while you change your clothes?
DAVID	Hey, I wore this special for you.
MA	I've seen it, it's cute, now put it away.
DAVID	Yeah, but . . .
MA	[*Pointing*] March.

DAVID   [*Exiting*] Now I know where Arnold got his technique.

MA   Cute kid. [*Calling out*] David? Where do you keep the phone numbers?

DAVID   [*Off*] In the phone book.

MA   A little too cute. Oy, Arnold, what have you got yourself into now? [*Finds book*] Here it is. Right on top. Must get used a lot. [*Starts to dial . . .*] David? What name shall I give them?

DAVID   What?

MA   Who shall I say is being excused? [*No response*] Your last name!

DAVID   [*Sticking his head in*] Beckoff, of course.

MA   Really? That's quite a coincidence. Have you and Arnold ever compared notes to see if there's any family relation?

DAVID   I'm his son. What more relation could there be? [*Arnold steps out of the bathroom.*]

MA   You're his what?

DAVID   His son. [*Arnold goes right back into the bathroom.*] Would you like that drink now?

The lights black out, music plays in the dark for a moment. It should be the Hartz Mountain Canaries singing "The Blue Danube Waltz."

Scene 2

Later that afternoon. The stage is exactly as it was before (except deserted). Ed lets himself in with his key. He enters carrying a small paper bag and newspaper.

ED   Hello? Anybody home?

A platter flies across the room from the hallway and just misses his head, smashing on the wall. It is followed by Arnold.

ARNOLD   Deserter! Defector! Duty dodger! Ditching your post at the first sign of battle, you backstabbing, betraying, ball-breaking, Buttercup! How could you leave me unprotected? You Avoider! Abstainer! Abandoner! Absconderer!

ED   Absconderer?

ARNOLD   If the shoe fits . . . Where have you been?

ED   Buying milk.

ARNOLD   For nine hours?

ED   I was on the express line. What happened?

ARNOLD   Happened? What could possibly have happened? My mother
          walked through that door and within three minutes managed
          to insult the plane ride, the bus ride, Women's Lib, the
          apartment, Manhattan, my personal hygiene, sense of hu-
          mor, afghan, smoking, stenciling and cockroaches. And, oh,
          you'll love this: She accused me of breaking up your marriage.

ED   You're kidding?

ARNOLD   She practically called me a homewrecker. O.K., so far so
          good. We finally sat down to chat when who should walk
          through the door, but the Patron Saint of Truants himself:
          Champ David. My mother gets a gander at him and goes,
          "What a sweet child. And whose little boy are you?" Giving
          the long awaited cue to my sweet little angel lamb to turncoat
          'round and point his every available finger at me.

ED   Oops.

ARNOLD   Did you say, "Oops"? No, Ed, "Oops" is when you fall down
          an elevator shaft. Oops is when you skinny-dip in a school of
          piranha. Oops is for accidentally douching with Drano. No,
          Ed, this was not an "Oops". This was a (STRANGLED
          SCREAM)!

ED   Cut the dramatics and tell me what happened.

ARNOLD   I'm telling you, nothing happened.

ED   Nothing?

ARNOLD   As in, "Not a thing." Dear David went atwitter to his room,
          mother went to my room, and I sat in the bathroom making
          toilet paper flowers and flushing them down the drain. Three
          hours I flowered and flushed, flowered and flushed, till Thank
          God, I ran out of paper. Forced from my Autumn Beige Tiled
          retreat, I called a truce for lunch. It was eaten in silence. No
          one even chewed. (You ever gum down a hamburger?) After

lunch David announced he was going back to school and my mother volunteered to walk him.

ED   Where are they now?

ARNOLD   I haven't the smoggiest. Knowing David, he's probably fuming over some pin-ball machine. I was gonna look for him but it's better if he makes it home on his own.

ED   That's very sensible.

ARNOLD   Not at all. But what would I say if I did find him? And the mother? . . . I don't know where she could be.

ED   "Leave them alone and they'll come home . . ."

ARNOLD   ". . . Dragging a noose behind them." Help me with dinner.

ED   A quick trip to the men's room and I'll set the table.

ARNOLD   You'll have to borrow a plunger from next-door, first. A thousand sheets really do last longer. [*Picking up the broken china*] Look at this, you broke my favorite platter.

ED   I broke?

ARNOLD   Come on, get going. And don't go disappearing on me again.

ED   I'll be right back. [*Exits*]

[*The phone rings. Arnold rushes to it.*]

ARNOLD   Hello? . . . Oh, hi, Murray. . . . No, I've been home all day. . . . Because I was in the bathroom . . . Yes, all day. You wanna sue me? . . . Look, Murr, I ain't got time to tear a herring with you now. You got somethin' to say? Say it. . . . Rocco who? Rocco DiGemma? The one with the leatherette tee-shirts? . . . Yeah, I know him. What about him? . . . You told him I'd do what?!!!?. . . . uh huh. . . . uh huh. . . . uh huh . . . uh huh . . . and then?. . . . uh huh. . . . uh huh . . . uh huh . . . uh huh . . . uh huh . . . Listen, Marie, [*At this point Ma and David enter happily*], you can call that poor excuse for a rubber creep back and tell him . . . [*He sees them.*] . . . tell him I've got a previous engagement. Thanks for calling. Bye bye. [*Hangs up*]

MA   [*Removing her jacket*] Who was that, dear?

ARNOLD   [*Puzzled*] It was Murray. He wanted me to do a favor for a friend.

MA   What did he want you to do?

ARNOLD   . . . Babysit. You were together?

DAVID   I took your mother to school with me.

MA   They were very nice. They let me sit in the back. He does very well; when he stays awake.

DAVID   Then I took her to play pinball.

MA   You weren't worried, were you?

ARNOLD   What, me worry?

DAVID   Hey, Alfred E., what's for dinner? [*Heads to kitchen*]

MA   Would you like to go out? My treat.

ARNOLD   I've started dinner here. But if you'd rather . . .

MA   No, we'll go out tomorrow. Besides, my feet are screaming for my slippers.

ED   [*Enters with plunger*] Well, look who's here.

MA   Hello, Ed. How was your day?

ED   Fine . . . thank you, Mrs. Beckoff. And yours?

MA   Surprisingly pleasant, once it was settled into. [*Exiting. To David*] After you do your homework I'll teach you how to play chess.

DAVID   [*With a can of soda*] Homework? Is she kidding? Hey, Arnold, we got a chess set?

ARNOLD   Top shelf of your closet.

DAVID   Thanks. Hi Ed. [*Exits*]

ED   And you were worried. [*Goes toward bathroom*]

ARNOLD   I wasn't worried. I was concerned. [*Ed exits.*]

MA   [*Enters in bunny slippers like Arnold's*] Give me an apron and put me to work.

ARNOLD   That's alright, Ma. Ed's gonna help.

MA   Oh, I wondered what the plunger was for. Listen, if I'm
           gonna die of ptomaine, it'll be from something I made my-
           self. [*Holding up a potato*] What do you want done with
           these?

ARNOLD   I was going to bake them, but if I could twist your
           arm . . . ?

MA   You want my Latkes?

ARNOLD   I'd love your Latkes.

MA   Then you'll get my Latkes.

ED   [*Entering*] All fixed.

ARNOLD   Thanks, Ed.

DAVID   [*Off*] Hey, Arnold? I can't find the chess board.

ARNOLD   Coming [*Exits*] Be back.

MA   [*Trying to draw Ed in*] You like Latkes, Ed?

ED   I don't know. I never had it.

MA   Them. You're in for a treat.

ED   I couldn't help noticing, you've got slippers like Arnold's.
           Mind if I ask who gave them to whom?

MA   [*Modeling them*] You like my slippers? Aren't they Chick?
           Arnold gave them to me. You know what they say; In matters
           of taste, there is none.

ED   I see where Arnold gets his wit.

MA   That and his appetite are from me. But the face?; he's his
           father's son. He's got his heart too. Always a soft touch. Tell
           me, Ed, what do you think of Arnold taking in this boy?

ED   I think it's wonderful.

MA   You do? Frankly, I'm not wild for it. But look, it's only for a
           few more weeks, so what harm could it do?

ED   Ooops.

MA   [*Calling to Arnold*] Arnold? You have Matzoh Meal?

ARNOLD   [*Enters*] Yeah, I'll get it for you.

MA   [*Proud*] He has Matzoh Meal. Did I bring him up right? [*David enters with a book, sits down on the couch and begins to read.*]

ARNOLD   Here you go, Ma. You need eggs?

MA   Two please. And an onion?

ED   [*Looking agog at David*] Are you doing homework?

DAVID   Nah. I'm just readin' somethin' from school.

MA   Arnold's father used to love my Latkes. But his favorite was my Potato Soup. You remember how he liked it, Arnold?

ARNOLD   I remember.

MA   It wasn't potato soup like you think; made with vegetables and cream. What he liked was: You took a potato, boiled it in water, threw in a bissel salt and pepper and that was Potato Soup. Arnold used to call it, "Daddy's Potato Water." You remember?

ARNOLD   Yes, Ma.

MA   We were Depression babies. You understand? Whether you have to or not, you carry that through your life. The tastes, the smells . . . They bring back a cozy feeling of a time you don't quite remember. You know what I'm talking?

ED   I think so.

MA   Good. 'Cause I don't. [*Arnold hugs her.*] What's that for?

ARNOLD   I'm glad you're here.

MA   Me too, Tatalah.

ED   [*To David*] I didn't know you could read.

DAVID   I just look at the pictures.

ED   What is it?

DAVID   Some garbage for English.

ED   What?

DAVID   A poem. I don't know. [*Reading and mispronouncing the* word *"Gaol"*] "The Ballad of Reading Gaol" by Oscar Wilde.

ED   [*Correcting*] That's gaol, like in j-a-i-l.

DAVID   That ain't what it says.

ED   That's the British spelling.

ARNOLD   [*From memory*] "Yet each man kills the thing he loves, By each let this be heard, Some do it with a bitter look, Some with a flattering word, The coward does it with a kiss, The brave man with a sword."

ED   Very good.

MA   What? You think I raised a dope?

ARNOLD   We had to learn it in High School. Y'know, I still get shivers when I think of that poor man going through all that pain and torment just to write a cliche.

DAVID   What's a cliche?

ARNOLD   The sincerest form of flattery.

DAVID   [*To Ed*] Was that a joke?

ARNOLD   [*Coming out of kitchen*] Did your teacher happen to mention how Oscar Wilde came to be imprisoned?

DAVID   Maybe. Who listens?

ARNOLD   He was in jail for being gay.

DAVID   No, I think I would'a remembered that.

MA   [*Embarrassed*] Arnold, I can't find the oil.

ARNOLD   In a minute, Ma. See, ten years earlier, the Parliament passed a law against homosexuality. And Oscar Wilde had this young lover named . . .

MA   Arnold, could you please give me a hand?

ARNOLD   Just a second. His name was Lord Alfred.

DAVID   Royalty, huh?

ED   [*To Ma*] Anything I can help you with?

MA   No, thank you, Ed.

ARNOLD   Now, Lord Alfred's father found out about them and started causing scenes in public; chasin' 'em outta hotels and stuff. But the straw that broke the dam was a note sent to Wilde's hotel. It said, "To Oscar Wilde who poses as a Sodomite."

MA   For God's sake, Arnold. Could you change the subject?

ARNOLD   *[Annoyed]* I'll finish later. *[Goes back to kitchen]*

ED   Here, we'll read the poem together and I'll explain anything you don't understand.

DAVID   I want the rest of the dish. *[Ed kicks him.]* Ouch, that hurt. *[David and Ed read quietly and we hear the conversation from the kitchen.]*

ARNOLD   I wish you wouldn't interfere like that; it's very embarrassing.

MA   Excuse me, but listening to that is very embarrassing.

ARNOLD   I'm sorry you feel that way, but I have a responsibility to his education.

MA   I am sure that the people who put him here did not have that kind of education in mind.

ARNOLD   The people who put him here had exactly that kind of education in mind. And I'll thank you not to interfere.

MA   I am only suggesting that you should consider the huge responsibility you've taken on here.

ARNOLD   You think I'm unaware of it?

MA   Then act like it. You should be setting an example for the boy.

ARNOLD   And I'm not?

MA   Not when you talk like that, you're not. You've got to consider what you say to him for the remaining time. He's at an impressionable age. After all it's only for a few more months.

ARNOLD   *[Ed and David stop.]* What's for a few more months?

MA   He's here on a nine-month program, right? And he's already been here six months, so . . .

ARNOLD   And what do you think happens then?

MA   He leaves.

DAVID   No, you misunderstoo . . . [*Ed kicks him again.*] Ow! This
            is getting serious.

ARNOLD   There seems to be misinterpretation afoot. Yes, David is here
            on a nine-month program, but after that, if we agree and the
            Bureau of Child Welfare allows, I will legally adopt David.
            And believe me, Ma, if I have anything to say about it, he's
            not leaving.
            [*Ma tries to say something, she is angry, confused, frustrated.
            She throws down whatever is in her hands and storms out. We
            hear the door slam.*]

ARNOLD   That was an "Ooops."

ED   I thought so.

ARNOLD   [*To David*] What'd you tell her?

DAVID   I didn't say nothin'.

ARNOLD   You certainly got a way without words. Well, kids, wish me
            luck.

DAVID   You goin' in there?

ARNOLD   Anybody got any suggestions?

DAVID   Don't look at me.

ED   Sorry, I'm just the babysitter.

ARNOLD   Somber times inspire your whimsicality. I'll remember that.

ED   And don't forget to write.

DAVID   We'll be in the next room; so talk loud.

ARNOLD   Thanks. [*Deep breath*] Well, here goes everything. [*He exits,
            we hear a knock on the door, then the door opens and closes.
            Ed and David jump up and rush to hallway.*]

DAVID   You hear anything?

ED   Sssshhhh.

DAVID   [*Going to kitchen*] Ah, he stalled too long. They're gonna
            need time to warm up again. Let's eat.

ED   I can't hear a thing. This is ridiculous; a grown man listening at a hallway. I should go right up to the door. [*He exits.*]

DAVID   [*Shouting*] You want a sandwich?

ED   [*Runs back in*] Could you not yell like that?

DAVID   [*Whispers*] Hear anything?

ED   No.

DAVID   Told ya'. Have a sandwich. We'll know when they get goin'.

ED   You're taking this very calmly. I'm more curious than you, it seems.

DAVID   Looks that way, don't it.

ED   What'd you tell her, anyway?

DAVID   A little of this, a little of that. What's the difference? You know how it is with grown-ups: They only hear what they wanna. [*He listens.*] Hang on, we're about to get a bulletin. [*Ma enters as if she rushed away. She sits on couch. Arnold follows and stands staring at her.*]

DAVID   Care to repose and repast?

ED   [*Grabs David*] Come on, Kissinger. I'll teach you how to play chess.

DAVID   Wait, my sandwich.

ED   [*Pulling him off*] You'll concentrate better on an empty stomach.

ARNOLD   [*Sits next to her. Pause*] Is this it? We gonna sit and stare into space?

MA   You want I should do a Bubble Dance?

ARNOLD   I need a cigarette. [*He gets one.*]

MA   Frankly, Arnold, you've done a lot of crazy things, but this . . . ?

ARNOLD   Adopting David is not a crazy thing. It's a wonderful thing that I'm very proud of.

MA   If you're so proud how come you were too ashamed to tell your mother? Everything else you tell me. You shove your sex-life down my throat like aspirin; every hour on the hour. But six months he's been here and not a word. Why?

ARNOLD   I don't know.

MA   So what's new?

ARNOLD   Ma . . . Y'know, you're not the easiest person in the world to talk to.

MA   What did I say? Do I tell you how to run your life? Let me tell you something, my son: I learned long ago that no matter what I said or how I felt you and your brother were going to do just as you pleased anyway. So, I wouldn't say a word. On purpose! You want to know why you didn't tell me about this? I'll tell you why: Because you knew it was wrong.

ARNOLD   That's not true.

MA   No?

ARNOLD   No!

MA   Why then?

ARNOLD   . . . I don't know.

MA   You would if you'd listened.

ARNOLD   This isn't something I decided to do overnight. We put in our application more than two years ago.

MA   Who "we"?

ARNOLD   Alan and I.

MA   The two of you were going to do this together?

ARNOLD   That was the idea.

MA   Now I've heard everything.

ARNOLD   That's what I love about you; you're so open minded.

MA   Alright. So, Alan's not here. Why's the kid?

ARNOLD   Because with everything else I forgot about the application. Then, one day, the phone rang. It was the foster parent program and they had David for us. I told them what happened to Alan and they said I could probably take David anyway.

MA   And you said, "send him on over."

ARNOLD   Not at first. But then I thought it all through, called them back and said yes. . . . On a trial basis.

MA   I'm glad you got a money-back guarantee, but you still haven't told me why you wanted him.

ARNOLD   Because I was tired of widowing.

MA   Wida-whating?

ARNOLD   Widowing. Widow-ing. It's a word of Murray's.

MA   And a nice one at that. What does it mean?

ARNOLD   You know.

MA   No, I don't know.

ARNOLD   Widowing . . . feeling sorry for myself, cursing everytime I passed a couple walking hand in hand, watching Tear Jerkers on T.V. knowing they could only cheer me up. Christ, of all the things going down here, I was sure that was the one thing I wouldn't have to explain.

MA   How should I know about Whatchamacallit? Did you ever say a word to me?

ARNOLD   I didn't think I had to. Christ, it's only been three years since daddy died.

MA   Wait, wait, wait, wait, wait. Are you trying to compare my marriage with you and Alan? [*Haughty and incensed*] Your father and I were married for thirty-five years, had two children and a wonderful life together. You have the nerve to compare yourself to that?

ARNOLD   [*Scared*] That's not what I mean, I'm talking about the loss.

MA   What loss did you have? You fooled around with some boy . . . ? Where do you come to compare that to a marriage of thirty-five years?

ARNOLD   You think it doesn't?

MA   Come on, Arnold. You think you're talking to one of your pals?

ARNOLD   Ma, I lost someone that I loved very much . . .

MA   So you felt bad. Maybe you cried a little. But what would you
            know about what I went through? Thirty-five years I lived
            with that man. He got sick, I brought him to the hospital and
            you know what they gave me back? I gave them a man . . .
            they gave me a paper bag with his watch, wallet and wedding
            ring. How could you possibly know what that felt like? It took
            me two months until I could sleep in our bed alone, a year to
            learn to say "I" instead of "we." And you're going to tell me
            you were "widowing." How dare you!

ARNOLD   You're right, Ma. How dare I. I couldn't possibly know how it
            feels to pack someone's clothes in plastic bags and watch the
            garbage pickers carry them away. Or what it feels like to
            forget and set his place at the table. How about the food that
            rots in the refrigerator because you forgot how to shop for
            one? How dare I? Right, Ma? How dare I?

MA   [*Starting over his speech and continuing until her exit*] May
            God strike me dead! Whatever I did to my mother to deserve
            a child speaking to me this way. The disrespect! I only pray
            that one day you have a son and that he'll talk to you like this.
            The way you talk to me.

ARNOLD   [*Over her speech*] Listen, Ma, you had it easy. You have
            thirty-five years to remember, I have five. You had your chil-
            dren and friends to comfort you, I had me! My friends didn't
            want to hear about it. They said, "What're you gripin' about?
            At least you had a lover." 'Cause everybody knows that queers
            don't feel nothin'. How dare I say I loved him? You had it
            easy, Ma. You lost your husband in a nice clean hospital, I lost
            mine out there. They killed him there on the street. Twenty-
            three years old laying dead on the street. Killed by a bunch of
            kids with baseball bats. [*Ma has fled the room. Arnold contin-
            ues to rant.*] Children. Children taught by people like you.
            'Cause everybody knows that queers don't matter! Queers
            don't love! And those that do deserve what they get! [*He
            stops, catches his breath, sits down*] Whatever happened to
            good ole' American Momism and apple pie?

DAVID   [*Sticking his head out from the hall*] Could you keep it down?
            There's people tryin' to concentrate.

ARNOLD   [*Laughing*] Sorry.

DAVID   Round one over?

ARNOLD   I really lost control. I didn't mean to say any of that. But it came pouring out; I felt like I was fighting for my life.

DAVID   [*Coming close*] This is highly flattering: A duel to the death over li'l ole me.

ARNOLD   Don't overdramatize. I do enough of that for both of us.

DAVID   [*Hug*] I think you're wonderful.

ARNOLD   Where's Uncle Ed?

ED   [*Sticking his head out*] Present. Is round one over?

ARNOLD   We've called a cease fire to re-group.

DAVID   Can we eat now?

ARNOLD   Why don't you two go out for something?

ED   How about you?

ARNOLD   Don't know why, but I ain't hungry. Go on.

ED   You're not going back in there, are you?

ARNOLD   I can't leave things like this.

ED   You're very brave.

ARNOLD   I'm very stupid. None of this would've happened if I'd been honest all along.

ED   Or dishonest all along.

ARNOLD   That's not for me. Get going.

ED   [*Intimate*] Let me stay. We can all talk together.

DAVID   You want us to bring something back for you?

ARNOLD   [*To David*] No, thanks. [*To Ed*] No, thanks.

DAVID   [*His jacket on*] Put a candle in the window when it's clear to come home. We'll wait on the bench.

ARNOLD   [*Hugging him*] I'll do that.

ED   [*At the door*] What'll it be; pizza?

DAVID   You paying?

ED   Sure.

DAVID   Then I know this intimate little French restaurant . . .
            [*Exit*]

ARNOLD   [*Takes a deep breath*] Round two. [*Sits on couch, feet up*] Yoo
            hoo, Mrs. Bloom! It's safe to come out. David and Ed went
            for a walk and we've got the whole place to fight in.

MA   [*Off*] Enjoy yourself. I'm going to bed.

ARNOLD   Ma, I'm sorry I lost my temper.

MA   Ha! I'm glad you're sorry.

ARNOLD   Please come out here. We can't talk like this.

MA   [*In doorway*] You don't want to talk, you want to fight. But I
            don't fight with my children. In your life did you ever hear
            your father and I fight? No. And do you know why? I'll tell
            you why: Because all my childhood I listened to fights. My
            father fought with my mother, my mother fought with my
            brother, my mother fought with me . . . When I married
            your father I told him, "Jack, I'll talk, but I won't fight." And
            did you ever hear us fight? No. And now you know why.

ARNOLD   You wanna sit down?

MA   [*Wandering over to the couch*] I'm sitting.

ARNOLD   Alright . . .

MA   [*Warning*] And don't holler at me. People say things they
            don't mean when they holler and you've already said quite
            enough.

ARNOLD   I won't holler. You just hit a raw nerve. We won't discuss
            Alan. Only David.

MA   So discuss.

ARNOLD   Why don't you tell me what you already know, and we'll go
            on from there.

MA   [*Trying*] I don't know anything.

ARNOLD   You spent the day with him. He must've said something.

MA   Let me think. He's an orphan . . .

ARNOLD   •He's not an orphan.

MA   He said he was an orphan.

ARNOLD   Well, he's not. He was a battered child. They took him away
          from his parents. This is his third foster home. The first
          brought him back. The second he ran away from. So. . . .

MA   So, he's a liar.

ARNOLD   He's not a liar . . .

MA   This isn't going to work.

ARNOLD   Come on, we're finally getting somewhere . . .

MA   How do you expect me to sit here and discuss this insanity?

ARNOLD   You're right, this isn't going to work.

MA   Arnold, Arnold, what do you know from raising a child?

ARNOLD   What's to know? Whenever I have a problem I simply imag-
          ine how you would solve it, and do the opposite.

MA   [*Standing*] Is this what you invited me up here for? To insult
          me and spit on your father's grave?

ARNOLD   For cryin' out . . . Will you please sit down?

MA   [*Sitting*] Don't holler. I'm sitting. I don't know why, but I'm
          sitting.

ARNOLD   Alright. Now we're going to talk about David. Not Alan, not
          daddy, just David. And we're going to stay calm.

MA   Ha!

ARNOLD   I give up.

MA   Arnold, darling, open your eyes. Don't you see how ridiculous
          this is? I've been here less than a day, already I've seen you let
          him miss school, hang out on the street, go out without
          dinner . . .

ARNOLD   This is hardly a typical day.

MA   You wanna talk or make excuses?

ARNOLD   This isn't Little Lord Fauntleroy we're talking about here. If
          this kid decided I was coming down too hard on him, he'd

pack and take off and I'd never get him back again. That sweet looking little boy knows how to make more money in a night than you and I could make in a week.

MA   So you let him run wild?

ARNOLD   No. But I don't beat him up either. I teach him. I advise him, I try to set an example for him . . .

MA   Some example. Arnold, look, you live the life you want. I put my fist in my mouth, I don't say a word. This is what you want. But think about the boy. He likes you. He told me he loves you. He sees you living like this . . . don't you think it's going to affect him?

ARNOLD   Ma, David is gay.

MA   But he's only been here six months!

ARNOLD   He came that way.

MA   No one comes that way.

ARNOLD   What an opening.

MA   By you everything is a joke.

ARNOLD   Don't you understand: the whole purpose of placing him here was for him to grow up with a positive attitude about his homosexuality.

MA   That's it. [*Stands*] I'm finished. The world has gone completely mad and I'm heading south for the summer.

ARNOLD   You make it very difficult to have an intelligent conversation.

MA   You want an intelligent conversation? Do what I do: talk to yourself. It's the only way.

ARNOLD   You think this is easy for me? Look; my hands are shaking. I've been like this for days knowing you'd be coming and we'd have to talk about this.

MA   Because you knew I'd show you how wrong you are.

ARNOLD   I'm not wrong.

MA   No? Tell me something: How old was your friend Alan when you met him?

ARNOLD   Seventeen.

MA   Seventeen. Seventeen and you were doing God knows what
          together. Now tell me; how old is this "son" of yours?

ARNOLD   I have no intention of sleeping with him if that's what you're
          driving at.

MA   I had no intention of having a homosexual for a son. So, look
          where intentions get you. Arnold, do what you want. You
          want to live like this? *Gay gezzintah hait.* I don't care any-
          more. You're not going to make me sick like you did your
          father.

ARNOLD   I made my father sick?

MA   No; he was thrilled to have a fairy for a son! You took a
          lifetime of dreams and threw them back in his face.

ARNOLD   What lifetime of dreams? He knew I was gay for fourteen
          years.

MA   What? You think you walk into a room, say, "Hi Dad, I'm
          queer," and that's that? You think that's what we brought you
          into the world for? Believe me, if I'd known I wouldn't have
          bothered. God should tear out my tongue, I should talk to my
          child this way. Arnold, you're my son, you're a good person, a
          sensitive person with a heart, *kennohorrah*, like your father
          and I try to love you for that and forget this. But you won't let
          me. You've got to throw me on the ground and rub my face in
          it. You haven't spoken a sentence since I got here without the
          word "Gay" in it.

ARNOLD   Because that's what I am.

MA   If that were all you could leave it in there [*Points to bedroom*]
          where it belongs; in private. No, you're obsessed by it. You're
          not happy unless everyone is talking about it. I don't know
          why you don't just wear a big sign and get it over with.

ARNOLD   [*Bordering on hysteria*] I don't know what to say to you. I
          really don't. I'm not trying to throw it in your face but it is
          what I am and it's not just a matter of who I sleep with.
          [*Crosses to her*] Ma, try to imagine the world the other way
          around. Imagine that every movie, book, magazine, T.V.
          show, newspaper, commercial, billboard told you that you

should be homosexual. But you know you're not and you know that for you this is right . . .

MA   Arnold, stop already. You're talking crazy.

ARNOLD   You want to know what's crazy? That after all these years I'm still sitting here justifying my life. That's what's crazy.

MA   You call this a life? This is a sickness! But this is what you've chosen for yourself.

ARNOLD   [*Deep breath, one last try*] Ma, look: I'm gay. I don't know why. I don't think anyone does. But that's what I am. For as far back as I can remember. Back before I knew it was different or wrong . . .

MA   You have not heard a word I've said.

ARNOLD   [*Losing control*] I know you'd rather I was straight but I am not! Would you also rather I had lied to you? My friends all think I'm crazy for telling you. They'd never dream of telling their parents. Instead they cut their parents out of their lives. And the parents wonder, "Why are my children so distant?" Is this what you'd rather?

MA   But it doesn't have to be our every conversation either.

ARNOLD   You want a part in my life? I am not going to edit out the things you don't like!

MA   [*Scared*] Can we end this conversation?

ARNOLD   No. There's one more thing you've got to understand. You made fun of my crocheting before. You think it's a cute little effeminate thing I do. Let me tell you something; I have taught myself to sew, cook, fix plumbing, do taxes, build furniture . . . I can even pat myself on the back when necessary. All so I don't have to ask anyone for anything. There is nothing I need from anyone except love and respect. And anyone who can't give me those two things has no place in my life. [*Breath*] You are my mother, and I love you. I do. But if you can't respect me . . . Then you've got no business being here.

MA   You're throwing me out?

ARNOLD   What I'm trying to . . .

MA   You're throwing me out! Isn't that nice? Listen Mister, you
              get one mother in this world. Only one. Wait. Just you wait.
              [*Ma exits to bedroom. Arnold is still as the next scene begins.*
              The lights slowly crossfade.]

Scene 3

A bench in the park below. Immediately following. If possible the bench
should be played on the couch. Through the use of Gobos and projections it
is conceivable to create the night-time park atmosphere on the apartment set.
David and Ed enter talking, eating hotdogs.

DAVID   How's your hotdog, Big Spender?

ED   Been years since I bought one of these off the street. I just
              remembered why.

DAVID   Teach you to forget your wallet. [*David sits on bench.*]

ED   C'mon, lazy. I gotta walk this thing off.

DAVID   We're supposed to wait here. [*Pointing up*] Look. You can see
              our windows from here. Almost didn't take the apartment
              because of it.

ED   You lost me.

DAVID   Arnold never brung you here? This is where it happened.

ED   I didn't know.

DAVID   Yeah, here. They were walking back toward the street, Alan
              and the other guy when the kids jumped out from behind
              these bushes. You can see; no way to run. Must've happened
              too quick anyway. Alan died right off, but the other guy
              crawled out to the street.

ED   I know.

DAVID   You can see a stain on the sidewalk in the daytime.

ED   Arnold showed you this?

DAVID   The day I moved in. At first I figured he was tryin' to scare me
              outta goin' into the park at night. I mean, I didn't know him
              from shit and here he takes me out, first day, and shows me
              some dried up blood on the sidewalk. I figured him for a nut-

case. Like maybe he had a case against the world or somethin'. I mean, havin' a bunch of piss-offs take out your lover for kicks . . . I could understand him bein' crazy. So, I felt sorry for him, but just passed it off. Then about a week later we were watchin' the news on T.V. and there was this protest march; a bunch of Jews marchin' against Nazis. They had these signs that said, "Never Again" and "We Remember." And I looked over at Arnold and he was like cryin' real soft, and just like that I connected. I knew why he showed me this.

ED	No candle in the window yet.
DAVID	Give 'em time, they got a lotta yellin' to catch up on.
ED	That's one thing I can do without hearing any more of today. I saw Laurel this afternoon.
DAVID	Oh, yeah? What'd she want?
ED	[*Realizing to whom he's talking*] Oh, nothing.
DAVID	Sure.
ED	Really.
DAVID	You don't have to tell me.
ED	It was nothing. Really.
DAVID	Hey, it's cool. You don't have to tell me. It ain't like we're old friends or nothing. After all, what am I to you?
ED	It was nothing. She just wanted to know if I was thinking of coming back.
DAVID	And you told her no.
ED	How do you know?
DAVID	I know.
ED	Frankly, I haven't made up my mind yet.
DAVID	You won't go back.
ED	Can we change the subject?
DAVID	Sure. So, now that you and Laurel are washed up, you gonna start shoppin' around?

ED   Well, since I haven't yet decided, then I haven't yet decided.

DAVID   Don't think about it too long or you'll wind up like Arnold.

ED   And that's bad?

DAVID   Arnold goes out to work and shop. That's all and that ain't
            healthy.

ED   You say that like you mean it.

DAVID   Who knows more about sex and its effect on mental health
            than me? Got any idea how many couches I've been laid out
            on? [*Ed smirks.*] Psychiatrically speaking. Starting when they
            turned my folks in I've had Freudian Analysis, Primal Analy-
            sis, Gestalt Analysis, Handwriting Analysis, Scream Therapy,
            Dream Therapy, Aversion Therapy and EST. When they
            finally ran outta cures to put me through, they stamped my
            file "Hopelessly Homo," shook my hand, wished me luck and
            shipped me off to Arnold. So I picked up plenty of know how
            on my journey down the "Leatherette Road."

ED   Knowing and doing are two different things. You're only
            fifteen.

DAVID   Guess you don't read the *New York Times*. Seems no matter
            how many petitions they sign, they just can't get God to raise
            the age of puberty to eighteen. Kids have sex. But that's
            another subject.

ED   It certainly is.

DAVID   Bottom line is, here's Arnold: Attractive, sensitive, intelli-
            gent, a great conversationalist, pretty good cook, and he's
            living like an old Italian widow.

ED   So?

DAVID   So it's time for a change. Don't you think?

ED   Maybe.

DAVID   Got any suggestions?

ED   None I'd care to discuss with a fifteen-year-old.

DAVID   And you called him a bigot? Look, I ain't askin' for no
            miracles. Though I must say I'd be proud to call you Daddy.
            I'm simply suggestin' you could both use a little T.E.N.

ED   T.E.N.?

DAVID   Tension Easing Nookie. Sex is very therapeutic.

ED   So you've said.

DAVID   What do you say?
            [*Arnold enters carrying two hot dogs like a wedding bouquet.*]

ARNOLD   [*a la Kate Hepburn*] Hello Mother. Hello Father. The frank-
            furters are in bloom again. [*Examines them*] Such a strange
            flower. Suitable for any occasion. I wore one on my wedding
            day, and now I place them here in memory of something that
            has . . . I don't know when to stop, do I? I brought sup-
            plies.

ED   [*Holding his stomach*] We had the same idea. They're poison.

DAVID   [*Grabbing two*] And so unfilling.

ARNOLD   Found your wallet on the table. Thought you might be hun-
            gry.

DAVID   Round two over?

ARNOLD   Two, three, four, five . . .

DAVID   Who won?

ARNOLD   When I left we both knew who won. Now only Robert
            Browning does. Ed, would you mind if I spoke to Champ
            alone?

ED   [*Embarrassed*] Oh, sure.

DAVID   No, stay. I want witnesses.

ED   It's O.K. Is it clear on the front?

ARNOLD   Should be. Got your key?

ED   [*Checks*] Yeah. I'll see you both later, then.

ARNOLD   Thanks, Ed. [*He exits.*]

DAVID   That was lousy. He wanted to help.

ARNOLD   I don't need his help, thank you. [*Pause*] Things got pretty
            "padded cell" up there.

DAVID   Yeah? [*Aloof*]

ARNOLD   You had to sit here, didn't you? I'm sorry I didn't tell her about you before. But believe me, it's not 'cause I was ashamed.

DAVID   Glad to hear it.

ARNOLD   My mother has a certain picture of what I should be doing with my life, and it's very hard for her to adjust to all the curves I throw in.

DAVID   Forge on.

ARNOLD   Alright. I knew that even if I told her about you, even before you came to live with me, that sooner or later we'd have this showdown. It has nothing to do with you. It's just her last go-for-broke campaign to straighten out my life.

DAVID   And?

ARNOLD   I asked her to leave.

DAVID   You're good at that.

ARNOLD   But you've got to understand that whatever happens between my mother and me has nothing to do with us.

DAVID   Come on, Arnold. This ain't Ed you're talking to. Whatever goes down with you two is exactly what will happen with us.

ARNOLD   How do you figure that?

DAVID   'Cause you're just like her.

ARNOLD   You wouldn't say that if you'd heard what went on up there.

DAVID   I know what goes on with mothers. Remember, you're my fourth. You think it's different 'cause we're both gay. But it's the same trip.

ARNOLD   No offense, Angel Puss, but you're mistaken.

DAVID   Think so? What would you do if I met a girl, came home and told you I was straight?

ARNOLD   If you were happy, I'd be happy.

DAVID   Bull-China! Here you are, workin' your butt off showin' me all the joys of gay life, givin' me the line on dignity and self-respect . . . You tellin' me you wouldn't wonder where you went wrong?

ARNOLD   Not if you were sure that that's what you wanted.

DAVID   Yeah, I see the way you treat Ed. The guy keeps tellin' you
            he's Bi and all you keep doin' is callin' him a Closet Case.

ARNOLD   See, you don't know what you're talking about. I'd be per-
            fectly willing to believe he's Bi if just once he thought about
            the person he was with before he considered what sex that
            person was.

DAVID   How could anybody do that? You ever meet someone and not
            know what sex they were?

ARNOLD   That's not what I mean . . .

DAVID   I know what you mean and it's just as dumb. [*Arnold tries to
            speak.*] Shut up and let me finish. I stay with you because I
            want to. Dig? I really like living with you. I even like the way
            you try to mother me. But you can really be a shithead about
            things. But, you make me feel like I got a home. And a bunch
            of other assorted mushy stuff I don't want to get into here.
            But, Arnold, I'm tellin' you now: I'll walk if you try to use me
            as an excuse for sitting home alone, or to pick a fight with
            your mother or with Ed. Hey, you do what you gotta do. I
            ain't judgin'. Just don't blame anybody but yourself if you get
            my drift. [*Pause*] You get my drift? [*Arnold nods.*] I come
            down too heavy? [*Shakes his head*] Still want me to stay?
            [*Arnold nods.*] Alright. Now we're dancin'.

ARNOLD   I ever tell you, I think you're swell?

DAVID   [*Standing*] Break this up. I got school tomorrow.

ARNOLD   [*Standing*] You go on ahead. I need an airing.

DAVID   Want company?

ARNOLD   Go on. I'll be up.

DAVID   O.K. See you later.

ARNOLD   David? You're not, are you?

DAVID   What?

ARNOLD   [*Embarrassed*] Straight?

DAVID   What would you do if I was?

ARNOLD   Kill you.

DAVID   [*Laughs*] Nice to know you care. [*Starts to leave*]

ARNOLD   Watch how you cross the street.
         [*The lights fade down and out.*]

Scene 4

Several hours later. The apartment. The lights are out, the couch unfolded and Ed is asleep in it. Arnold enters in a robe from the bathroom heading toward the kitchen, weaving, with an empty glass in his hand.

ED   [*Waking*] Huh? What?

ARNOLD   It's me. Go to sleep.

ED   Arnold? Oh. [*Trying to wake*] What time is it?

ARNOLD   Almost six. Go to sleep.

ED   I waited up for you.

ARNOLD   I see.

ED   You want to talk?

ARNOLD   No. Go to sleep.

ED   I don't want to go to sleep.

ARNOLD   So don't go to sleep.

ED   You just get home?

ARNOLD   A while ago.

ED   I didn't hear you. Where'd you go? [*No response*] She said she's leaving.

ARNOLD   I know. I tripped over her bags on my way in.

ED   She didn't want to stay the night, but she couldn't get a flight out until morning. When I came in she was walking out to spend the night in the airport. I got her calmed down a little. [*Pause*] She'd stay if you asked her.

ARNOLD   Go to sleep.

ED   Stop telling me to go to sleep.

ARNOLD   Alright, go to hell! [*Sorry*] Want a drink?

ED   Sure, white wine. [*Arnold shoots a look.*] Juice. [*As Arnold makes the drinks*] You know, I saw Laurel today. That's where I went. I don't think she's overjoyed with the separation. She told me she's pregnant. She's not, but she said she was to see if I'd go back to her . . . if she was. God. The things that ran through my mind. Baby carriages, walks in the park, my folks playin' with it . . . Quite a sensation. I guess I would've gone back if she was. But then . . . I don't know.

ARNOLD   I hope you didn't tell her that.

ED   Of course I did. After five years of marriage, I'm not going to start lying to her now.

ARNOLD   [*Numb*] What'd she say?

ED   She said she could be . . . if I came back. [*Pause*] She thinks we're sleeping together. Funny, huh? Laurel and your mother thinking the same thing. Maybe they know something we don't. [*Clears his throat*] I suppose it's her way of expressing anger. Laurel. Not your mother. Though I have seen happier women than her. Your mother, that is. [*Arnold is now sitting on the bed. He snickers.*] What's so funny?

ARNOLD   Seems like everytime I turn around here we are: Arnold and Ed in bed together.

ED   Talking.

ARNOLD   Talking. Me with a lump in my throat and you with a foot in your mouth.

ED   Why? What'd I say?

ARNOLD   Don't ask me. I stopped listening years ago.

ED   I don't see what I said that's . . .

ARNOLD   It was nothing. Pay me no mind; I'm drunk.

ED   Look, I know I'm not the most sensitive person in the world . . .

ARNOLD   Ed, take a note: Never fish for compliments in polluted waters.

ED   Are you really drunk?

ARNOLD   I hold it well, don't I? A trick I learned in finishing school. It's done with mirrors. You think I'm here in bed next to you but actually I'm asleep under a table in a bar on Forty-third.

ED   [*Amused*] This is the first time I've ever seen you drunk.

ARNOLD   Well get a good look, Leon, 'cause I'm dryin' out in the morning.

ED   Arnold Beckoff drunk.

ARNOLD   Blottoed, plastered and plotzed . . . incorporated.

ED   Why'd you get drunk?

ARNOLD   [*Knocking on Ed's head*] Hello? Anybody home? Sometimes you really frighten me.

ED   [*Offering his arms and shoulder*] Care to talk about it?

ARNOLD   Sure. Why should the neighbors have all the fun? [*Lies back*] I had a genuinely superior motive for drinking this much. Don't tell nobody, but I'm a pushover when I'm drunk. And I thought that if I got good and looped I'd repent and ask my mother to stay. It worked, too. Until I got a peek at her sitting in there on the bed with her "Holier Than Thou" attitude and her "Merry Martyr" smile. The way she acts you'd think she and God went to school together. She thinks I hate her. I know the way her mind works and she thinks I hate her.

ED   I'm sure she knows you don't.

ARNOLD   Oh, no, she does. She thinks I hate her and everything she stands for. And I don't, for the life of me, know how to tell her that what I want more than anything is to have exactly the life she had. With a few minor alterations. My parents . . . They were something together. In all the years they were married the only time they were separated was for two days while my mother was in the hospital. And my father . . . He wouldn't even get into bed without her. He spent both nights on a chair in the living room. And the way they made my brother and me feel; like we were the smartest, handsomest, most talented, most important two people in the world. Didn't matter what we did, good or bad, it was the best. And she thinks she did something wrong.

ED   Are you really a pushover when you're drunk?

ARNOLD   Earth to Ed. Earth to Ed. Come in please. [*Ed giggles.*]
          You've got your own problems don't'cha? C'mon, spill your
          guts.

ED   David said you haven't gone out since Alan died.

ARNOLD   We're talking about you now.

ED   I can understand you not wanting to at first, but still. You
          could at least go out for a few drinks, take a quick trip to the
          backroom. No harm in that.

ARNOLD   You may not understand this, but I want more out of life than
          meeting a pretty face and sitting down on it. That answer
          your question?

ED   Graphically.

ARNOLD   I do my best.

ED   If I made a pass at you now . . . Would you let me?

ARNOLD   Alright, who spiked the orange juice?

ED   Actually, it's David's idea. He thinks you're pushing chastity
          too far. He says it's unhealthy.

ARNOLD   This is the first time I've been seduced in the guise of preven-
          tive medicine.

ED   I told him I'd consider it.

ARNOLD   What a friend.

ED   I didn't mean it that way.

ARNOLD   You never do.

ED   I mean, this is not exactly what I want.

ARNOLD   I came to the same conclusion myself. I think it was the
          wedding that gave you away.

ED   I didn't want that either. I mean, I did, but it turned out not
          to be what I want. In fact, it made me less sure than ever
          about what it is I do want.

ARNOLD   No problem. I've got a Sears catalogue you can flip through.
          If you see it there give a primal scream and I'll get it for your
          birthday.

ED   You're not being fair.

ARNOLD   I'm upset, uptight, and up to my nipples in Southern Com-
          fort. I'm sorry.

ED   Never mind.

ARNOLD   I said I'm sorry. You're trying to say something and I've got
          diarrhea of the mouth. Come on, I'll behave. I promise. [*No
          response*] Hey, this is Arnold here. You can tell me anything.

ED   I want another chance with you.

ARNOLD   Anything but that.

ED   Wait. Just think about it for a minute. It makes a lot of sense.
          We know each other so well, there'd be no surprises. We
          know what to expect from each other. You said yourself we
          have no secrets.

ARNOLD   What'd that kid of mine say to you?

ED   Just listen for a second. Laurel and I together . . . It wasn't
          enough. Obviously or I wouldn't be here. And that's the
          point: I am here. No matter what I do, I always end up back
          here, with you, in bed . . .

ARNOLD   Talking!

ED   Talking. But here. Arnold, the time I've spent here with you
          and David . . . it's been the closest thing to whatever it is I
          want. I feel wonderful here . . .

ARNOLD   "Don't care if the kid ain't mine, I wanna be the father of
          your baby." I saw that movie. I even read the book.

ED   Are you finished?

ARNOLD   Ed, please.

ED   Not five minutes ago it's what you said you wanted.

ARNOLD   I thought you weren't listening.

ED   I know you're upset about your mother.

ARNOLD   That's not it . . .

ED   O.K. so maybe it's too soon after Alan . . .

ARNOLD   Oh, Puh-lease!

ED   I'm asking you to think about it. That's all. Just think.

ARNOLD   Don't you know that I have? How thick can you possibly be?
          Can't you see that since you called that's all I've thought
          about? Five days ago you walked through the door and from
          that moment I've been playing the dutiful wife and mother
          to your understanding if distant father. And David? He's
          been having the time of his life playing baby.

ED   And it's been wonderful.

ARNOLD   It's been preposterous. It's a joke. Three grown men playing
          house!

ED   You think this is playing house? You have no idea what
          playing house is. Arnold, I love Laurel. That may sound a
          little strange considering the circumstances, but my feelings
          for her are genuine and just as strong now as when we got
          married. It has, however, become apparent that what we have
          is a friendship, not a marriage.

ARNOLD   That's a hell of a lot more than most people have.

ED   I'm almost forty, Arnold. Can you understand what that
          means? It means it's time for me to stop jerkin' around. I
          want more than a marriage which is at best purposeless,
          unfulfilling but perfectly acceptable. Now, whatever you
          think of us, you could never describe us like that.

ARNOLD   Not the perfect part anyway.

ED   Are you through making cracks?

ARNOLD   I just don't see what you think is here that you can't have
          with Laurel.

ED   To tell you the truth I'm not sure either. But there's some-
          thing that's kept me coming back . . .

ARNOLD   Are you forgetting why we broke up in the first place? You
          really think you could bring your friends here? You ready to
          introduce me to your parents as your lover and to David as *our*
          son? Ed. Angel, I just threw my mother—my *mother*—out of
          my house and all she wanted was to not talk about it. You
          think I'll ask less from you?

ED   I think it's time to find out.

ARNOLD   I don't know, Ed. Christ, I mean, I don't even know what this is supposed to be. I can't exactly buy a book or study some *Reader's Digest* article that's gonna tell me. All I know is whatever this is, it's not a Grade B imitation of a heterosexual marriage. See, I thought that Alan and David and I could find out together . . . so now . . .

ED   Let me help you find out. You, me and David.

ARNOLD   I can't.

ED   Why? You scared I'll walk out again? Of course I can't guarantee anything . . .

ARNOLD   That's not it.

ED   Then is it David? You afraid I'll hurt him?

ARNOLD   I know how you feel about him, I know you wouldn't.

ED   Then what, Arnold?

ARNOLD   [*Deep breath*] I am not Laurel.

ED   I'm counting on that.

ARNOLD   Go home, Ed.

ED   Are you crying?

ARNOLD   Leave me alone.

ED   I can't. Not with you like this. You need someone to talk to.

ARNOLD   [*Striking out*] I don't need anyone. Thank you.

ED   Well, maybe I do.

ARNOLD   Then go home. You've got a lovely wife who'd do anything for you. She can give you a home, a two-car garage, a child of your own, white picket fence . . . the whole shebang double dipped in chocolate and government approved. Go home, Ed. I ain't got nothin' like that here.

ED   You really believe that? [*Arnold nods.*] Your mother did quite a job on you. [*Teasing*] Hello? Anybody home? You're gonna make me say it, aren't you? Undemonstrative soul that I am, you're gonna make me say it.

ARNOLD   I don't want you to say anything.

ED   Oh no, I'll say it. I'm not ashamed, embarrassed maybe, but not ashamed. But I'll be damned if I say it to your back. [*Pulls Arnold over and pins him down*]

ARNOLD   Ed! For Chrissake!

ED   You ready? Now you better listen good 'cause I don't know when I'll get the guts to say it again.

ARNOLD   Ed, you're gonna wake my mother.

ED   So, let her hear. I hope they're both listening. Might as well let everyone know. Is everybody listening? O.K. Here goes. Arnold Beckoff . . . I love . . .

DAVID   [*Interrupting as he enters*] What the hell's going on in here?

ED   Perfect timing.

DAVID   [*Throwing on the lights: We can now see his black and blue eye.*] Oh, am I interrupting something? I hope, I hope, I hope.

ARNOLD   [*Straightening up his appearance*] You're not, you're not. What're you doing up at this hour?

DAVID   My alarm went off ten minutes ago. In case you lovebirds haven't noticed, it's morning.

ED   Jesus!

DAVID   Is this a closed marriage or can anybody join in?

ARNOLD   [*As David climbs into bed between them*] And baby makes three.

ED   My first pajama party.

DAVID   [*To Arnold*] You look awful. Didn't you sleep?

ARNOLD   Nary a wink, blink or nod.

ED   . . . Incorporated.

ARNOLD   Thank you.

ED   Don't mention it.

ARNOLD   Any news from the other camp?

DAVID   I heard shuffling. I think she's ready to leave.

ARNOLD   I'd better splash my face and get ready for the grand exit.

ED   [*As Arnold struggles to rise*] Need help?

ARNOLD   I think my battery's dead. Gimme a boost.
          [*They shove from behind, Arnold flies to his feet. Then, a la Mae West*] Thanks, boys. [*Exits into bathroom*]

DAVID   [*Anxiously*] Well?

ED   I struck out. He said no.

DAVID   You asked first? Don't you know anything? It don't mean nothin', anyway. Arnold always says no when you ask him a question. Then he thinks about it and . . . Watch. [*Calling out*] Hey, Arnold? You want breakfast?

ARNOLD   [*Off*] No, thanks.

DAVID   [*Counts to ten on his fingers.*] Now . . .

ARNOLD   [*Off*] David? Maybe I'll have an egg.

DAVID   Most contrary person I've ever met.

ED   [*Getting out of bed*] We better get dressed. They should be alone for the final round.

DAVID   I am dressed.

ED   Show off. Well, start the coffee while I catch up. [*Exits*]

DAVID   [*Heading to the kitchen*] Do you like pancakes?

ED   [*Off*] I love pancakes.

DAVID   Great. I'll make you some . . . when I learn to cook. [*He turns on the radio.*]

RADIO   Plaza 6-6654 with your requests. It's six fifty-four in the Big Apple on what looks to be a beautiful June day. And I'm here, with you, dedicated to the one you love. Now an Oldie by request, from Beulah to Robert and Michael. Guess she just can't make up her mind. Ha, ha. Alright, Beulah, here it is with love. [*Music begins*] Our number's Plaza 6-6654 and I'm waiting to play one for you. [*Music continues into the scene.*]

ARNOLD   [*Entering*] What're you listening to?

DAVID   One of those call-in shows, I think. Want me to change it?

ARNOLD   No, leave it. I ever tell you about the time Alan phoned in a
            request to one of those shows? They read the dedication
            wrong. He announced, "From Ellen to Arnold." He must'a
            thought it was a typo or somethin'.

DAVID   What song was it?

ARNOLD   "My Funny Valentine." [*David wretches.*] It was very Ro-
            mantic.

DAVID   Is your mother staying for breakfast?

ARNOLD   Ask her, not me. Has she shown her face yet?

DAVID   Nope.

ARNOLD   Go on in and see if she needs any help.

DAVID   [*Dramatically*] "Into the jaws of Death, Into the mouth of
            Hell!" Any message?

ARNOLD   No. [*David exits. Arnold folds the couch. Mother screams off-
            stage.*] Not again.

MA   [*Enters with David*] Arnold, did you see this eye? How could
            you let him walk around with a face like this? [*Drags him to
            the kitchen*] Come over here. I'm going to put some ice on it.

DAVID   Mrs. Beckoff, it's alright.

MA   Alright? You look like an ad for "I'd rather fight than switch."

ARNOLD   [*To David's rescue as Ed enters*] Ma, leave him alone. Ice
            won't help. He's had it for two days.

MA   What're you talking? I saw him yesterday . . .

ARNOLD   He covered it with make-up so he'd look nice for you.

DAVID   I'm O.K. Really. But thanks, anyway.

ED   C'mon, Champ. I'll buy you breakfast out.

DAVID   [*Surveying the scene*] Great. But I gotta do somethin' first.
            [*Towards bedroom*] I'll be out in a minute.

ED   [*Putting on his jacket*] I guess I'll see you later. [*To Ma*] It was
            a pleasure meeting you, Mrs. Beckoff.

MA   The pleasure was mine, Ed. I hope you and your wife come to

your senses. Couples must learn to live with conflict. After all,
a problem is never as permanent as a solution.

ED   Uh . . . Thank you. [*Shouting*] David? Hurry up.

ARNOLD   Aren't you going to wash up first?

ED   That's alright. I'm alright. [*Pause. Desperate*] David!!!

DAVID   [*Off*] I'm comin', already!

ARNOLD   [*Taking Ed aside*] Ed? What we were talking about before?
            Y'know, six years is a long time . . . I don't know. But we
            can talk.

ED   That's all I'm asking. [*Trying to control himself*] Good. Good.

DAVID   [*Enters with a big grin*] Here I is.

MA   You take care of that eye.

DAVID   I will. It was nice meeting you. [*To Ed*] Remember your
            wallet this time? [*Ed checks*] See you later, Arnold. [*Gives
            him a peck on the cheek*]

ARNOLD   Have a nice day. And don't come home before school's over!

DAVID   [*To Ed*] You look like someone kicked you in the head. [*They
            exit. David sticks his head back in*] And you two play like nice
            children. [*Out*]

ED   [*Off*] Yahoo!

ARNOLD   [*Holding back a laugh*] He likes the wallpaper. Covers a
            multitude of sins.

MA   [*Bringing her bags to the door*] I'll be leaving myself, now.

ARNOLD   You don't have to fly back to Florida. You could stay . . .

MA   With your brother? No. It's better if he doesn't know about
            this. I'll call him from Miami, tell him I changed my plans
            and couldn't make it up this week.

ARNOLD   I'm going to tell him what happened.

MA   [*Angry*] Do what you want. I don't care.

ARNOLD   Ma, it's important that he knows. He's part of this family too.

MA   What else do you want to do to me? What, Arnold, what?
            You want me to leave? I'm leaving. You want me to fight? I'm

too tired. You want me to change? I'm too old and I can't. I can't, I can't, I can't. So you do what you have to do, and I'll do what I have to do and I hope you're satisfied. [*Arnold groans*] If I had ever opened a mouth to my mother like you did to me, you'd be talking to a woman with a size six wedgie sticking out of her forehead. But I didn't raise my children like that. I wanted them to respect me because they wanted to. Not because I beat it in to them. Go now.

ARNOLD   Do we have to start this again?

MA   Yes. Because you can't put all the blame on me. It's not fair. Some of it was my fault, but not all. You think I didn't know about you, Arnold? Believe me, I knew. And not because you told me. I didn't need you to tell me. I knew but I said no. I hoped . . . What's the difference, I knew and I turned my back. But I wasn't the only one. There are other things you should have told me. You opened a mouth to me about your friend Alan . . . How was I supposed to know?

ARNOLD   Why? You would have understood?

MA   Maybe. Maybe not. You can't know for sure. But I flew up for the funeral and you never said a word.

ARNOLD   So you could've done what?: Tell me he's better off dead?

MA   Or maybe I could've comforted you. Told you what to expect. You and your "widowing." [*She turns to leave, stops, takes a breath. One last try.*] And about this Ed: You love him?

ARNOLD   I don't know. I think so.

MA   Like you loved Alan?

ARNOLD   No. They're very different. Alan loved all my faults; my temper, my bitchiness, my fat . . . He looked for faults to love. And Ed? Ed loves the rest. And really, who needs to be loved for their virtues? Anyway, it's easier to love someone who's dead; they make so few mistakes.

MA   You've got an unusual way of looking at things, Arnold Beckoff.

ARNOLD   Runs in the family. Ma, I miss him so much.

MA   Give yourself time, Arnold. It gets better. But, Arnold, it won't ever go away. You can work longer hours, adopt a son,

fight with me . . . whatever, it'll still be there. But that's alright. It becomes part of you, like wearing a ring or a pair of glasses. You get used to it and it's good . . . because it makes sure you don't forget. You don't want to forget him, do you? [*Arnold shakes his head*] So, it's good. [*Pause*] I guess that's what I would have said . . . [*The phone rings*] if I'd known. You'd better answer that. It may be something with that . . . son of yours.
[*Arnold goes to the phone. As soon as he's turned his back, Ma slips out the door with her bags. Arnold doesn't notice.*]

ARNOLD   [*Answering*] Hello . . . Hi Murray . . . What? . . . The radio? It's on. . . . Alright, hang on. [*He puts the phone down and goes to the radio, turning up the volume.*] It's Murray, something about the radio.

RADIO   [*Mid-sentence*] . . . no, I've just checked with my producer who took the call and he's confirmed it. What a morning. Whatever is this world coming to? So, here it is, a dedication from David to Arnold with all his love . . .

          [*Music begins to play. It is Big Maybelle singing, "I Will Never Turn My Back On You."*]

ARNOLD   How do you like that? That's some kid I got there, huh? [*Turning*] You hear that, Ma? [*Sees she's gone*] Ma? [*Goes to door*] Ma?

Runs to window and looks out as the music plays. He turns toward the audience and listens to the song calmly. As the music ends, the lights fade and the curtain falls.

THE END

About the Author

Harvey Fierstein is a recipient of the Rockefeller Foundation Grant in Playwrighting, the Ford Foundation Grant for New American Plays, a CAPS Fellowship, a special OBIE Award for writing and acting, four *Villager* Awards, the *Soho News* Commendation for best New American Play, a Corporation For Public Broadcasting Grant, the Fund For Human Dignity Award, two Drama Desk Nominations, the George Oppenheimer/Newsday Playwrighting Award, an Association of Comedy Artists Award, and the Hull/ Warriner Award from the Dramatists Guild.

With a Fine Arts degree from Pratt Institute, Mr. Fierstein began his writing career in 1973. Beyond his current Broadway presentation, *Torch Song Trilogy,* he has two new works slated for production this coming season: *Spookhouse,* a full length play for Off Broadway, and the musical comedy, *La Cage aux Folles* with music and lyrics by Jerry Herman, to be directed by Arthur Laurents. Mr. Fierstein is also now writing an original teleplay for P.B.S. entitled, *Kaddish and Old Men.*

Born June 6, 1954 in Brooklyn, Harvey began his acting career as a founding member of The Gallery Players, a Brooklyn based community theater group which is still in existence. He made his professional acting debut with Andy Warhol in 1971 at La Mama ETC. With more than 60 productions to his credit, Harvey has also appeared in numerous films. Most recently as the voice of the Devil in the television film, *The Demon Murder Case.*

As owner of two dogs (Georges and Bubbie), and a rabbit (Arnold), Harvey's interests are varied. In his spare time between writing and acting he collapses.